On Trial

On Trial

*Being a Summary of Eyewitness Reports
Concerning the Early Church*

By Luke the Physician

PARAPHRASED BY KENNETH TAYLOR

ILLUSTRATED BY JAMES McILRATH

OUR SUNDAY VISITOR, INC./*Huntington, Indiana*

Dedication to Theophilus   vii

1   Choosing an Apostle   1
2   The Spirit Comes   4
3   Peter Cures a Lame Man   8
4   Before the Sanhedrin   12
5   Pious Frauds   15
6   False Witnesses   19
7   The First Martyr   21
8   Persecution   23
9   An Unlikely Convert   27
10 The Sheet in the Sky   31
11 Peter's Vision Explained   35
12 Saved by an Angel   38
13 'A Light to the Gentiles'   42
14 Preaching on the Run   46
15 Dissension and Decision   49
16 Earthquake   53
17 Idols at Athens   57
18 Accused by the Jews   60
19 The Tradesmen Riot   63
20 A Last Good-bye   67
21 Saved by Soldiers   70
22 Paul Tells His Story   75
23 The Plot to Kill Paul   78
24 Two Years in Prison   81
25 Paul Appeals to Caesar   84
26 Before King Agrippa   87
27 Shipwreck   90
28 Under House Arrest   95

About the Author / About Paul the Apostle   98

5717

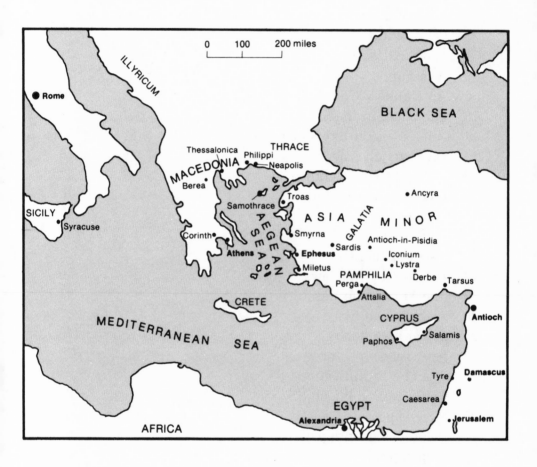

Most Excellent Theophilus,

DEAR FRIEND WHO LOVES GOD: In my first letter I told you about Jesus' life and teachings and how he returned to heaven after giving his chosen apostles further instructions from the Holy Spirit. During the forty days after his crucifixion, he appeared to the apostles from time to time, actually alive, and proved to them in many ways that it was really he himself they were seeing. And on these occasions he talked to them about the Kingdom of God.

—LUKE

Choosing an Apostle

IN ONE OF THESE MEETINGS Jesus told his apostles not to leave Jerusalem until the Holy Spirit came upon them in fulfillment of the Father's promise, a matter he had previously discussed with them.

"John baptized you with water," he reminded them, "but you shall be baptized with the Holy Spirit in just a few days."

And another time when he appeared to them, they asked him, "Lord, are you going to free Israel from Rome now and restore us as an independent nation?"

"The Father sets those dates," he replied, "and they are not for you to know. But when the Holy Spirit has come upon you, you will receive power to testify about me with great effect, to the people in Jerusalem, throughout Judea, in Samaria, and to the ends of the earth—about my death and resurrection."

It was not long afterward that he rose into the sky and disappeared into a cloud, leaving them staring after him. As they were straining their eyes for another glimpse, suddenly two white-robed men were standing there among them. "Men of Galilee," they said, "why are you standing here staring at the sky? Jesus has gone away to heaven, and someday, just as he went, he will return!"

They were at the Mount of Olives when this happened, so now they walked the half mile back to Jerusalem and held a prayer meeting in an upstairs room of the house where they were staying.

Here is the list of those who were present at the meeting: Peter, John, James, Andrew, Philip, Thomas, Bartholomew, Matthew, James (son of Alphaeus), Simon (also called the Zealot), Judas (son of James), and the cousins of Jesus. Several women, including Jesus' mother, were also there.

This prayer meeting went on for several days. During this time, on a day when about 120 people were present, Peter stood up and addressed them. "My friends," he said, "it was necessary for the Scriptures to come true concerning Judas, who betrayed Jesus by guiding the mob to him, for this was predicted long ago by the Holy Spirit, speaking through King David. Judas was one of us, chosen to be an apostle, just as we were. He bought a field with the money he received for his treachery and, falling headlong there, he burst open, spilling out his bowels. The news of his death spread rapidly among all the people of Jerusalem, and they named the place the Field of Blood. King David's prediction of this appears in the Book of Psalms, where he says, 'Let his home become desolate with no one living in it.' And again, 'Let his work be given to someone else to do.'

"So now we must choose someone else to take Judas' place and to join us as witnesses of Jesus' resurrection. Let us select someone who has been with us constantly from our first association with the Lord—from the time he was baptized by John until the day he was taken from us into heaven."

The assembly nominated two men: Joseph Justus (also called Barsabbas) and Matthias. Then they all prayed for the right man to be chosen. "O Lord," they said, "you know every heart; show us which of these men you have chosen as an apostle to

2

replace Judas the traitor, who has gone on to his proper place."

Then they drew straws, and in this manner Matthias was chosen and became an apostle with the other eleven.

CHAPTER TWO

The Spirit Comes

SEVEN WEEKS HAD GONE BY since Jesus' death and resurrection, and the day of Pentecost had now arrived. As the believers met together that day, suddenly there was a sound like the roaring of a mighty windstorm in the skies above them, and it filled the house where they were meeting. Then what looked like flames or tongues of fire appeared and settled on their heads. And everyone present was filled with the Holy Spirit and began speaking in languages they didn't know, for the Holy Spirit gave them this ability.

Many godly Jews were in Jerusalem that day for the religious celebrations, having arrived from many nations. And when they heard the roaring in the sky above the house, crowds came running to see what it was all about, and the people were stunned to hear their own languages being spoken by the disciples.

"How can this be?" they exclaimed. "For these men are all from Galilee, and yet we hear them speaking all the native languages of the lands where we were born! Here we are—Parthians, Medes, Elamites, men from Mesopotamia,

4

Judea, Cappadocia, Pontus, Ausia, Phrygia, Pamphilia, Egypt, the Cyrene-language areas of Libya, visitors from Rome—both Jews and Jewish converts—Cretans, and Arabians. And we all hear these men telling in our own languages about the mighty miracles of God!"

They stood there amazed and perplexed. "What can this mean?" they asked each other.

But others in the crowd were mocking. "They're drunk, that's all!" they said.

Then Peter stepped forward with the eleven apostles and shouted to the crowd: "Listen, all of you, visitors and residents of Jerusalem alike! Some of you are saying these men are drunk! It isn't true! It's much too early for that! People don't get drunk by 9 A.M. No! What you see this morning was predicted centuries ago by the prophet Joel: 'In the last days,' God said,

> I will pour out my Holy Spirit upon all mankind, and your sons and daughters shall prophesy, and your young men shall see visions, and your old men dream dreams. Yes, the Holy Spirit shall come upon all my servants, men and women alike, and they shall prophesy. And I will cause strange demonstrations in the heavens and on the earth—blood and fire and clouds of smoke; the sun shall turn black and the moon blood-red before that awesome Day of the Lord arrives. But anyone who asks for mercy from the Lord shall have it and shall be saved.

"O men of Israel, listen!" Peter urged. "God publicly endorses Jesus of Nazareth by doing tremendous miracles through him, as you well know. But God, following his prearranged plan, let you use the Roman government to nail him to the cross and murder him. Then God released him from the horrors of death and brought him back to life again, for death could not keep this man within its grip. Speaking as if in the voice of Jesus, King David said:

5

I know the Lord is always with me. He is helping me. God's mighty power supports me. No wonder my heart is filled with joy and my tongue shouts his praises! For I know all will be well with me in death—you will not leave my soul in hell or let the body of your Holy Son decay. You will give me back my life, and give me wonderful joy in your presence.

"Dear brothers, think! David wasn't referring to himself when he spoke these words I have quoted, for he died and was buried, and his tomb is still here among us. But he was a prophet and knew God had promised with an unbreakable oath that one of David's own descendants would be the Messiah and sit on David's throne. David was looking far into the future and predicting the Messiah's resurrection and saying that the Messiah's soul would not be left in hell and his body would not decay. He was speaking of Jesus, and we all are witnesses that Jesus rose from the dead.

"And now he sits on the throne of highest honor in heaven, next to God. And just as promised, the Father gave him the authority to send the Holy Spirit—with the results you are seeing and hearing today.

"No, David was not speaking of himself in these words of his I have quoted, for he never ascended into the skies. Moreover, he further stated, 'God spoke to my Lord, the Messiah, and said to him, "Sit here in honor beside me until I bring your enemies into complete subjection." '

"Therefore I clearly state to everyone in Israel that God has made this Jesus you crucified to be the Lord, the Messiah!"

These words of Peter's moved them deeply, and they said to him and to the other apostles, "Brothers, what shall we do?"

And Peter replied, "Each one of you must turn from sin, return to God, and be baptized in the name of Jesus Christ for the forgiveness of your sins; then you also shall receive this gift, the Holy Spirit. For Christ promised him to each one of you who has been called by the Lord our God, and to your children, and even to those in distant lands!"

Then Peter preached a long sermon, telling about Jesus and strongly urging all his listeners to save themselves from the evils of their nation. And those who believed Peter were baptized—about 3,000 in all! They joined with the other believers in regular attendance at the apostles' teaching sessions, at the breaking of bread, and at prayer meetings. A deep sense of awe was on them all, and the apostles did many miracles.

And all the believers met together constantly and shared everything with each other, selling their possessions and dividing them among those in need. They worshiped together at the Temple each day, met in small groups in homes to break bread together, sharing their meals with great joy and thankfulness, and praising God. The whole city was favorable to them, and each day God added to them those who were being saved.

CHAPTER THREE

Peter Cures a Lame Man

PETER AND JOHN WENT to the Temple one afternoon to take part in the three o'clock daily prayer meeting. As they approached the Temple, they saw a man who had been lame from birth being carried along the street and laid beside the Temple gate—the one called the Beautiful Gate—as was his daily custom. As Peter and John were passing by, he asked them for some money.

They looked at him intently, and then Peter said, "Look here!"

The lame man looked at them eagerly, expecting a gift.

But Peter said: "We don't have any money for you! But I'll give you something else! I command you in the name of Jesus Christ of Nazareth, *walk!*"

Then Peter took the lame man by the hand and pulled him to his feet. And as he did, the man's feet and anklebones were healed and so strengthened that he came up with a leap, stood there a moment, and began walking! Then, walking, leaping, and praising God, he went into the Temple with them.

When the people inside saw him walking and heard him

praising God and realized that he was the lame beggar they had seen so often at the Beautiful Gate, they were inexpressibly surprised! They all rushed out to Solomon's Hall, where he was holding tightly to Peter and John! Everyone stood there, awed by the wonderful thing that had happened.

Peter saw his opportunity and addressed the crowd. "Men of Israel," he said, "what is so surprising about this? And why look at us as though we by our own power and godliness had made this man walk? For it is the God of Abraham, Isaac, Jacob, and of all our ancestors who has brought glory to his servant Jesus by doing this. I refer to the Jesus whom you rejected before Pilate, despite Pilate's determination to release him. You didn't want him freed—this holy, righteous one. Instead you demanded the release of a murderer. And you killed the Author of Life; but God brought him back to life again. And John and I are witnesses to this fact; for after you killed him, we saw him alive!

"Jesus' name has healed this man—and you know how lame he was before. Faith in Jesus' name—faith given us from God—has caused this perfect healing.

"Dear brothers, I realize that what you did to Jesus was done in ignorance; and the same can be said of your leaders. But God was fulfilling the prophecies that the Messiah must suffer all these things. Now change your mind and your attitude toward God, and turn to him so that he can cleanse away your sins and send you wonderful times of refreshment from the presence of the Lord and send Jesus your Messiah back to you again. For he must remain in heaven until the final recovery of all things from sin, as was prophesied from ancient times. Moses, for instance, said long ago: 'The Lord God will raise up a Prophet among you, who will resemble me! Listen carefully to everything he tells you. Anyone who will not listen to him shall be utterly destroyed.'

"Samuel and every prophet since have all spoken about what is going on today. You are the children of these prophets; and you are included in God's promise to your ancestors to bless the entire world through the Jewish race—that is the promise God gave to Abraham. And as soon as God has brought his servant to life again, he sent him first of all to you men of Israel, to bless you by turning you back from your sins."

CHAPTER FOUR

Before the Sanhedrin

WHILE THEY WERE TALKING to the people, the chief priests, the captain of the Temple police, and some of the Sadducees came over to them, very disturbed that Peter and John were claiming that Jesus had risen from the dead. They arrested them and, since it was already evening, jailed them overnight. But many of the people who heard their message believed it, with the result that the number of believers now reached a new high of about 5,000 men!

The next day it happened that the Council of all the Jewish leaders was in session in Jerusalem—Annas the High Priest was there, as were Caiaphas, John, Alexander, and others of the High Priest's relatives. So the two disciples were brought in before them.

"By what power or by whose authority have you done this?" the Council demanded.

Then Peter, filled with the Holy Spirit, said to them: "Honorable leaders and elders of our nation, if you mean the good deed done to the cripple, and how he was healed, let me clearly state to you and to all the people of Israel that it was done in the name and by the power of Jesus from Nazareth, the Messiah—the man you crucified but God raised to life again. It is by his authority that this man stands here healed. For Jesus the Messiah is the one referred to in the Scriptures when they speak of a 'stone discarded by the builders which became the capstone of the arch.' There is salvation in no one else. Under heaven there is no other name that men may call upon to save them."

When the Council saw the boldness of Peter and John, obviously uneducated nonprofessionals, they were amazed and realized what being with Jesus had done for them! And the Council could hardly discredit the healing when the man they had healed was standing right there beside them! So they sent Peter and John out of the Council chamber and conferred among themselves.

"What shall we do with these men?" they asked each other. "We can't deny that they have done a tremendous miracle; everybody in Jerusalem knows about it. But perhaps we can stop them from spreading their propaganda. We'll tell them that if they do it again, we'll really throw the book at them." So the Council called them back in and told them never again to speak about Jesus.

But Peter and John replied: "You decide whether God wants us to obey you instead of him! We cannot stop telling about the wonderful things we saw Jesus do and heard him say."

The Council then threatened them further. But they finally had to let them go because they didn't know how to punish them without starting a riot; for everyone was praising God for this wonderful miracle—the healing of a man who had been lame for forty years.

As soon as they were freed, Peter and John found the other disciples and told them what the Council had said. Then all the believers united in this prayer:

O Lord, Creator of heaven and earth and of the sea
and everything in them—you spoke long ago by the

Holy Spirit through our ancestor King David, your servant, saying: "Why do the heathens rage against the Lord, and the foolish nations make their little plots against Almighty God? The kings of the earth unite to fight against him and against the anointed Son of God!"

That is what is happening here in this city today! For Herod the king, Pontius Pilate the governor, and all the Romans—as well as the people of Israel—are united against Jesus, your anointed Son, your holy servant. They won't stop at anything that you in your wise power will let them do. And now, O Lord, hear their threats and grant to your servants great boldness in their preaching and send your healing power; and may miracles and wonders be done by the name of your holy servant Jesus.

After this prayer, the building where they were meeting shook, and they were all filled with the Holy Spirit and boldly preached God's message.

All the believers were of one heart and mind, and no one felt that what he owned was his own; everyone was sharing. And the apostles preached powerful sermons about the resurrection of the Lord Jesus, and there was warm fellowship among all the believers, and no poverty—for all who owned land or houses sold them and brought the money to the apostles to give to others in need.

For instance, there was Joseph (the one the apostles nicknamed Barney the Preacher! He was of the tribe of Levi, from the island of Cyprus). He was one of those who sold a field he owned and brought the money to the apostles for distribution to those in need.

CHAPTER FIVE

Pious Frauds

BUT THERE WAS A MAN named Ananias (with his wife, Sapphira) who sold some property and brought only part of the money, claiming it was the full price. (His wife had agreed to this deception.)

But Peter said: "Ananias, Satan has filled your heart. When you claimed this was the full price, you were lying to the Holy Spirit. The property was yours to sell or not, as you wished. And after selling it, it was yours to decide how much to give. How could you do a thing like this? You weren't lying to us but to God."

As soon as Ananias heard these words, he fell to the floor, dead! Everyone was terrified, and the younger men covered him with a sheet and took him out and buried him.

About three hours later his wife came in, not knowing what had happened. Peter asked her if she and her husband had sold their land at such and such a price?

"Yes," she replied, "we did."

And Peter said: "How could you and your husband even think of doing a thing like this—conspiring together to test the

Spirit of God's ability to know what is going on? Just outside that door are the young men who buried your husband, and they will carry you out too."

Instantly she fell to the floor, dead, and the young men came in and, seeing that she was dead, carried her out and buried her beside her husband. Terror gripped the entire church and all others who heard what had happened.

Meanwhile, the apostles were meeting regularly at the Temple in the area known as Solomon's Hall, and they did many remarkable miracles among the people. The other believers didn't dare join them, though, but all had the highest regard for them. And more and more believers were added to the Lord, crowds both of men and women. Sick people were brought out into the streets on beds and mats so that at least Peter's shadow would fall across some of them as he went by! And crowds came in from the Jerusalem suburbs, bringing their sick folk and those possessed by demons; and every one of them was healed.

The High Priest and his relatives and friends among the Sadducees, reacting with violent jealousy, arrested the apostles and put them in the public jail.

But an angel of the Lord came at night, opened the gates of the jail, and brought them out. Then he told them, "Go over to the Temple and preach about this Life!"

They arrived at the Temple about daybreak and immediately began preaching! Later that morning the High Priest and his courtiers arrived at the Temple, and, convening the Jewish Council and the entire Senate, they sent for the apostles to be brought for trial. But when the police arrived at the jail, the men weren't there, so they returned to the Council and reported, "The jail doors were locked, and the guards were standing outside, but when we opened the gates, no one was there!"

When the police captain and the chief priests heard this, they were frantic, wondering what would happen next and where it would all end. Then someone arrived with news that the men they had jailed were in the Temple, preaching to the people!

The police captain went with his officers and arrested them (without violence, for they were afraid the people would kill them if they roughed up the disciples) and brought them in before the Council.

"Didn't we tell you never again to preach about this Jesus?" the High Priest demanded. "And instead you have filled all Jerusalem with your teaching and intend to bring the blame for this man's death on us!"

But Peter and the apostles replied, "We must obey God rather than men. The God of our ancestors brought Jesus back to life again after you had killed him by hanging him on a cross. Then, with mighty power, God exalted him to be a Prince and Savior in order that the people of Israel would have an opportunity to repent and have their sins forgiven. And we are witnesses of these things, and so is the Holy Spirit, who is given by God to all who obey him."

At this, the Council was furious and decided to kill them. But one of their members, a Pharisee named Gamaliel (an expert on religious law, and very popular with the people), stood up and requested that the apostles be sent outside the Council chamber while he talked.

Then he addressed his colleagues.

"Men of Israel," he said, "take care what you are planning to do to these men! Some time ago there was that fellow Theudas, who pretended to be someone great. About 400 others joined him, but he was killed and his followers were harmlessly dispersed.

"After him, at the time of the taxation, there was Judas of Galilee. He drew away some people as disciples, but he also died and his followers scattered.

"And so my advice is, leave these men alone. If what they teach and do is merely on their own, it will soon be overthrown. But if it is of God, you will not be able to stop them, and you might even find yourselves fighting against God."

The Council accepted his advice, called in the apostles, had them beaten, then told them never again to speak in the name of Jesus, and finally let them go. They left the Council chamber rejoicing that God had counted them worthy to suffer dishonor for his name. And every day, in the Temple and in their home Bible classes, they continued to teach and preach that Jesus is the Messiah.

CHAPTER SIX

False Witnesses

BUT WITH THE NUMBER of believers growing rapidly, there were rumblings of discontent. Those who spoke only Greek complained that widows in their group were being discriminated against, that they were not being given as much food in the daily distribution as were the widows who spoke Hebrew. So the Twelve called a meeting of all the believers.

"We should spend our time preaching, not administering a feeding program," they said. "Now look around among yourselves, dear brothers, and select seven men, wise and full of the Holy Spirit, who are well thought of by everyone; and we will put them in charge of this business. Then we can spend our time in prayer, preaching, and teaching."

This sounded reasonable to the whole assembly, and they elected the following: Stephen (a man unusually full of faith and the Holy Spirit), Philip, Prochorus, Nicanor, Timon, Parmenas, and Nicolaus of Antioch (a gentile convert to the Jewish faith who had become a Christian).

These seven were presented to the apostles, who prayed for them and laid their hands on them in blessing.

God's message was preached in ever-widening circles, and the number of disciples increased vastly in Jerusalem; and many of the Jewish priests were converted too. Stephen, the man so full of faith and the power of the Holy Spirit, did spectacular miracles among the people.

But one day some of the men from the Jewish cult of the Freedmen started an argument with him, and they were soon joined by Jews from Cyrene; Alexandria, in Egypt; and the Turkish provinces of Cilicia and Ausia. But none of them could stand against Stephen's wisdom and spirit.

So they brought in some men to lie about him, claiming they had heard Stephen curse Moses—and even God.

This accusation roused the crowds to fury against Stephen, and the Jewish leaders arrested him and brought him before the Council. The lying witnesses testified again that Stephen was constantly speaking against the Temple and against the laws of Moses.

They declared, "We have heard him say that this fellow Jesus of Nazareth will destroy the Temple and throw out all of Moses' laws." At this point everyone in the Council chamber saw Stephen's face become as radiant as an angel's!

CHAPTER SEVEN

The First Martyr

THEN THE HIGH PRIEST asked Stephen, "Are these accusations true?"

At this point, Stephen begins a lengthy response that has puzzled many readers of the New Testament. He does not answer the accusations directly. Instead, he recounts the story of the Jewish people from the time of Abraham. But Stephen's history lesson is not without its point—a rather stinging one at that. A clear pattern emerges: time after time, the Israelis have rejected God's messengers; again and again, they have persecuted the prophets of the Lord.

Stephen's response begins quietly enough, but at the end it becomes a countercharge. Seeing that his own trial is a sham, Stephen speaks defiance to those sitting in judgment upon him. These are the same men who have forbidden the apostles to speak in Jesus' name. This is the Council that sought to crucify Jesus. The same Annas and Caiaphas are here. After level-

ing his own accusations against the Jewish leaders, Stephen concludes:

"You stiff-necked heathens! Must you forever resist the Holy Spirit? But your fathers did, and so do you! Name one prophet your ancestors didn't persecute. They even killed the ones who predicted the coming of the Righteous One—the Messiah, whom you betrayed and murdered. Yes, and you deliberately destroyed God's laws, though you received them from the hands of angels."

The Jewish leaders, stung to fury by Stephen's accusation, ground their teeth in rage. But Stephen, full of the Holy Spirit, gazed steadily upward into heaven and saw the glory of God, and Jesus standing at God's right hand. And he told his hearers, "Look! I see the heavens opened and Jesus the Messiah standing beside God at his right hand!"

Then they mobbed him, putting their hands over their ears and drowning out his voice with their shouts, and dragged him out of the city to stone him. The official witnesses—the executioners—took off their coats and laid them at the feet of a young man named Saul.

And as the murderous stones came hurtling at him, Stephen prayed, "Lord Jesus, receive my spirit." And he fell to his knees, shouting, "Lord, don't charge them with this sin." And with that, he died.

CHAPTER EIGHT

Persecution

SAUL WAS IN COMPLETE AGREEMENT with the killing of Stephen. And a great wave of persecution of the believers began that day, sweeping over the church in Jerusalem, and everyone except the apostles fled into Judea and Samaria. (But some godly Jews came and with great sorrow buried Stephen.) Saul was like a wild man, going everywhere to devastate the believers, even entering private homes and dragging out men and women alike and jailing them.

But the believers who had fled Jerusalem went everywhere, preaching the good news about Jesus! Philip, for instance, went to the city of Samaria and told the people there about Christ. Because of the miracles he did, crowds listened intently to what he had to say. Many evil spirits were cast out, screaming as they left their victims, and many who were paralyzed or lame were healed. So there was much joy in that city!

A man named Simon had formerly been a sorcerer there for many years; he was a very influential, proud man because of the amazing things he could do—in fact, the Samaritan people often spoke of him as the Messiah. But now they believed Philip's message that Jesus was the Messiah, and his words concerning the Kingdom of God; and many men and women were baptized. Then Simon himself believed and was baptized and began following Philip wherever he went, and he was amazed by the miracles Philip did.

When the apostles back in Jerusalem heard that the people of Samaria had accepted God's message, they sent down Peter and John. As soon as they arrived, they began praying for these new Christians to receive the Holy Spirit, for as yet he had not come upon any of them. For they had only been baptized in the name of the Lord Jesus. Then Peter and John laid their hands upon these believers, and they received the Holy Spirit.

When Simon saw this—that the Holy Spirit was given when the apostles placed their hands upon people's heads—he offered money to buy this power.

"Let me have this power too," he exclaimed, "so that when I lay my hands on people, they will receive the Holy Spirit!"

But Peter replied: "Your money perish with you for thinking God's gift can be bought! You can have no part in this, for your heart is not right before God. Turn from this great wickedness and pray. Perhaps God will yet forgive your evil thoughts—for I can see that there is jealousy and sin in your heart."

"Pray for me," Simon exclaimed, "that these terrible things won't happen to me."

After testifying and preaching in Samaria, Peter and John returned to Jerusalem, stopping at several Samaritan villages along the way to preach the good news to them too.

But as for Philip, an angel of the Lord said to him, "Go over to the road that runs from Jerusalem through the Gaza Desert, arriving around noon." So he did, and who should be coming down the road but the treasurer of Ethiopia, a eunuch of great authority under Candace the queen. He had gone to Jerusalem to worship at the Temple and was now returning in his chariot, reading aloud from the book of the prophet Isaiah.

The Holy Spirit said to Philip, "Go over and walk along

24

beside the chariot." So Philip ran over and heard what he was reading and asked, "Do you understand it?"

"Of course not!" the man replied. "How can I when there is no one to instruct me?" And he begged Philip to come up into the chariot and sit with him.

The passage of Scripture he had been reading from was this:

> He was led as a sheep to the slaughter, and as a lamb is silent before the shearers, so he opened not his mouth; in his humiliation, justice was denied him; and who can express the wickedness of the people of his generation? For his life is taken from the earth.

The eunuch asked Philip, "Was Isaiah talking about himself or someone else?"

So Philip began with this same Scripture and then used many others to tell him about Jesus.

As they rode along, they came to a small body of water, and the eunuch said, "Look! Water! Why can't I be baptized?"

"You can," Philip answered, "if you believe with all your heart."

And the eunuch replied, "I believe that Jesus Christ is the Son of God."

He stopped the chariot, and they went down into the water, and Philip baptized him. And when they came up out of the water, the Spirit of the Lord caught away Philip, and the eunuch never saw him again but went on his way, rejoicing. Meanwhile, Philip found himself at Azotus! He preached the good news there and in every city along the way as he traveled to Caesarea.

CHAPTER NINE

An Unlikely Convert

BUT SAUL, THREATENING with every breath and eager to destroy every Christian, went to the High Priest in Jerusalem. He requested a letter addressed to synagogues in Damascus, requiring their cooperation in the persecution of any believers he found there, both men and women, so that he could bring them in chains to Jerusalem.

As he was nearing Damascus on this mission, suddenly a brilliant light from heaven blazed all around him! He fell to the ground and heard a voice saying to him, "Saul, Saul! Why are you persecuting me?"

"Who is speaking, sir?" Saul asked.

And the voice replied: "I am Jesus, the one you are persecuting! Now get up and go into the city and await my further instructions."

The men with Saul stood speechless with surprise, for they heard the sound of someone's voice but saw no one! As Saul picked himself up off the ground, he found that he was blind. He had to be led into Damascus, where he remained three days, blind, going without food and water all that time.

Now there was in Damascus a believer named Ananias. The Lord spoke to him in a vision, calling, "Ananias!"

"Yes, Lord!" he replied.

And the Lord said, "Go over to Straight Street and find the house of a man named Judas and ask there for Saul of Tarsus. He is praying to me right now, for I have shown him a vison of a man named Ananias coming in and laying his hands on him so that he can see again!"

"But Lord," exclaimed Ananias, "I have heard about the terrible things this man has done to the believers in Jerusalem! And we hear that he has warrants with him from the chief priests, authorizing him to arrest every believer in Damascus!"

But the Lord said, "Go and do what I say. For this man is my chosen instrument to take my message to the nations and before kings, as well as to the people of Israel. And I will show him how much he must suffer for me."

So Ananias went over and found Saul and laid his hands on him and said, "Brother Saul, the Lord Jesus, who appeared to you on the road, has sent me so that you may be filled with the Holy Spirit and get your sight back."

Instantly (it was as though scales fell from his eyes) Saul could see, and he was immediately baptized. Then he ate and was strengthened. After staying with the believers in Damascus for a few days, he went at once to the synagogue to tell everyone there the good news about Jesus—that he is indeed the Son of God!

All who heard him were amazed. "Isn't this the same man who persecuted Jesus' followers so bitterly in Jerusalem?" they asked. "And we understand that he came here to arrest them all and take them in chains to the chief priests."

Saul became more and more fervent in his preaching, and the Damascus Jews couldn't withstand his proofs that Jesus was indeed the Christ.

After a while the Jewish leaders determined to kill him. But Saul was told about their plans, that they were watching the gates of the city day and night, prepared to murder him. So, during the night, some of his converts let him down in a basket through an opening in the city wall!

When he arrived in Jerusalem, he tried to meet with the believers, but they were all afraid of him. They thought he was faking! Then Barnabas brought him to the apostles and told them how Saul had seen the Lord on the way to Damascus, what the Lord had said to him, and all about his powerful preaching in the name of Jesus. Then they accepted him, and after that he was constantly with the believers and preached boldly in the name of the Lord. But then some Greek-speaking Jews with whom he had argued plotted to murder him. However, when the other believers heard about his danger, they took him to Caesarea and then sent him to his home in Tarsus.

Meanwhile, the church was left in peace throughout Judea, Galilee, and Samaria, and grew in strength and numbers. The believers learned how to walk in the fear of the Lord and in the comfort of the Holy Spirit.

Peter traveled from place to place to visit them, eventually coming to the believers in the town of Lydda. There he met a man named Aeneas, who had been paralyzed and bedridden for eight years.

Peter said to him: "Aeneas! Jesus Christ has healed you! Get up and make your bed." And he was healed instantly. Then, when they saw Aeneas walking around, all the residents of Lydda and Sharon turned to the Lord.

In the city of Joppa there was a woman named Dorcas ("Gazelle"), a believer who was always doing kind things for others, especially for the poor. About this time she became ill and died. Her friends prepared her for burial and laid her in an upstairs room. But when they learned that Peter was nearby at Lydda, they sent two men to beg him to return with them to Joppa. This he did; and as soon as he arrived, they took him upstairs where Dorcas lay. The room was filled with weeping widows who were showing one another the coats and other garments Dorcas had made for them. But Peter asked them all to leave the room. Then he knelt and prayed. Turning to the body, he said, "Get up, Dorcas," and she opened her eyes! And when she saw Peter, she sat up! He gave her his hand and helped her up. Then he called in the believers and widows, presenting her to them.

The news raced through the town, and many believed in the Lord. And Peter stayed a long time in Joppa, living with Simon the tanner.

CHAPTER TEN

The Sheet in the Sky

IN CAESAREA there lived a Roman army officer, Cornelius, a captain of an Italian regiment. He was a godly man, deeply reverent, as was his entire household. He gave generously to charity and was a man of prayer. While wide awake one afternoon, he had a vision—it was about three o'clock—and in this vision he saw an angel of God coming toward him.

"Cornelius!" the angel said.

Cornelius stared at him in terror. "What do you want, sir?" he asked the angel.

And the angel replied: "Your prayers and charities have not gone unnoticed by God! Now send some men to Joppa to find a man named Simon Peter, who is staying down by the shore with Simon the tanner, and ask him to come and visit you."

As soon as the angel was gone, Cornelius called two of his household servants and a godly soldier, who was one of his personal bodyguards, told them what had happened, and sent them off to Joppa.

The next day, as they were nearing the city, Peter went up on the flat roof of his house to pray. It was noon and he was hungry, but while lunch was being prepared, he fell into a trance. He saw the sky open and a great canvas sheet, suspended by its four corners, settle to the ground. In the sheet were all sorts of animals, snakes, and birds forbidden to the Jews for food.

Then a voice said to him, "Go, kill and eat any of them you wish."

"Never, Lord!" Peter declared. "I have never in all my life eaten such creatures, for they are forbidden by our Jewish laws."

The voice spoke again: "Don't contradict God! If he says something is kosher, then it is."

The same vision was repeated three times. Then the sheet was pulled up again to heaven. Peter was very perplexed. What could the vision mean? What was he supposed to do?

Just then the men sent by Cornelius had found the house and were standing outside at the gate, inquiring whether this was the place where Simon Peter lived!

Meanwhile, as Peter was puzzling over the vision, the Holy Spirit said to him: "Three men have come to see you. Go down and meet them and go with them. All is well. I have sent them."

So Peter went down. "I'm the man you're looking for," he said. "Now what is it you want?"

Then they told him about Cornelius, the Roman officer, a good and godly man well thought of by the Jews, and how an angel had instructed him to send for Peter to come and tell him what God wanted him to do.

So Peter invited them in and lodged them overnight. The next day, accompanied by some other believers from Joppa, he went with them.

They arrived in Caesarea the following day. Cornelius was waiting for Peter and had called together his relatives and close friends to meet him. As Peter entered his home, Cornelius fell to the floor before him in worship.

But Peter said, "Stand up! I'm not a god!"

So he got up and they talked together for a while and then went in where the others were assembled.

Peter told them: "You know it is against the Jewish laws for me to come into a gentile home like this. But God has shown me in a vision that I should never think of anyone as inferior. So I came as soon as I was sent for. Now tell me what you want."

Cornelius replied: "Four days ago I was praying as usual at this time of the afternoon, when suddenly a man was standing before me clothed in a radiant robe! He told me: 'Cornelius, your prayers are heard, and your charities have been noticed by God! Now send some men to Joppa and summon Simon Peter, who is staying in the home of Simon, a tanner, down by the shore.' So I sent for you at once, and you have done well to come so soon. Now here we are, waiting before the Lord, anxious to hear what he has told you to tell us!"

Then Peter replied: "I see very clearly that the Jews are not God's only favorites! In every nation he has those who worship him and do good deeds and are acceptable to him. I'm sure you have heard about the good news for the people of Israel—that there is peace with God through Jesus, the Messiah, who is Lord of all creation. This message has spread all through Judea, beginning with John the Baptist in Galilee. And you no doubt know that Jesus of Nazareth was anointed by God with the Holy Spirit and with power, and he went around doing good and healing all who were possessed by demons, for God was with him.

"And we apostles are witnesses of all he did throughout Israel and in Jerusalem, where he was murdered on a cross. But God brought him back to life again three days later and showed him to certain witnesses God had selected beforehand—not to the general public but to us who ate and drank with him after he rose from the dead. And he sent us to preach the good news everywhere and to testify that Jesus is ordained of God to be the Judge of all—living and dead. And all the prophets have written about him, saying that all those who believe in him will

33

have their sins forgiven through his name."

Even as Peter was saying these things, the Holy Spirit fell upon all those listening! The Jews who came with Peter were amazed that the gift of the Holy Spirit would be given to gentiles too! But there could be no doubt about it, for they heard them speaking in tongues and praising God.

Peter asked, "Can anyone object to my baptizing them, now that they have received the Holy Spirit just as we did?" So he did, baptizing them in the name of Jesus, the Messiah. Afterward, Cornelius begged him to stay with them for several days.

Peter's Vision Explained

Soon THE NEWS reached the apostles and other brothers in Judea that gentiles also were being converted! But when Peter arrived back in Jerusalem, the Jewish believers argued with him.

"You had fellowship with gentiles and even ate with them," they accused.

Then Peter told them the whole story. "One day in Joppa," he said, "while I was praying, I saw a vision—a huge sheet, let down by its four corners from the sky. Inside the sheet were all sorts of animals, reptiles, and birds that we are not to eat. And I heard a voice say, 'Kill and eat whatever you wish.'

" 'Never, Lord,' I replied. 'For I have never yet eaten anything forbidden by our Jewish laws!'

"But the voice came again. 'Don't say it isn't right when God declares it is!'

"This happened *three times* before the sheet and all it contained disappeared into heaven. Just then three men who had come to take me with them to Caesarea arrived at the house where I was staying! The Holy Spirit told me to go with them and not to worry about their being gentiles! These six brothers here accompanied me, and we soon arrived at the home of the man who had sent the messengers. He told us how an angel had appeared to him and told him to send messengers to Joppa to find Simon Peter. 'He will tell you how you and all your household can be saved,' the angel had told him.

"Well, I began telling them the good news, but as I was getting started with my sermon, the Holy Spirit fell on them, just as he fell on us at the beginning! Then I thought of the Lord's words, when he said, 'Yes, John baptized with water, but you shall be baptized with the Holy Spirit.' And since it was *God* who gave these gentiles the same gift he gave us when we believed in the Lord Jesus Christ, who was I to argue?"

When the others heard this, all their objections were answered and they began praising God! "Yes," they said, "God has given to the gentiles, too, the privilege of turning to him and receiving eternal life!"

Meanwhile, the believers who fled from Jerusalem during the persecution after Stephen's death traveled as far as Phoenicia, Cyprus, and Antioch, scattering the good news, but only to Jews. However, some of the believers who went to Antioch from Cyprus and Cyrene also gave their message about the Lord Jesus to some Greeks. And the Lord honored this effort, with the result that large numbers of these gentiles became believers.

When the church at Jerusalem heard what had happened, they sent Barnabas to Antioch to help the new converts. When he arrived and saw the wonderful things God was doing, he was filled with excitement and joy, and he encouraged the believers to stay close to the Lord, whatever the cost. Barnabas was a kindly person, full of the Holy Spirit and strong in faith. As a result, large numbers of people were added to the Lord.

Then Barnabas went on to Tarsus to hunt for Paul. When he found him, he brought him back to Antioch; and both of them stayed there for a full year, teaching the many new converts. (It was there at Antioch that the believers were first called "Christians.")

During this time some prophets came down from Jerusalem to Antioch, and one of them, a man named Agabus, stood up in one of the meetings to predict by the Spirit that a great famine was coming upon the land of Israel. (This prophecy was fulfilled during the reign of Claudius.) So the believers decided to send relief to the Christians in Judea, each giving as much as he could. This they did, consigning their gifts to Barnabas and Paul to take to the elders of the church in Jerusalem.

CHAPTER TWELVE

Saved by an Angel

ABOUT THAT TIME King Herod moved against some of the believers and killed the apostle James (John's brother). When Herod saw how much this pleased the Jewish leaders, he arrested Peter during the Passover celebration and imprisoned him, placing him under the guard of sixteen soldiers. Herod's intention was to deliver Peter to the Jews for execution after the Passover. But earnest prayer was going up to God from the Church for Peter's safety all the time he was in prison.

The night before he was to be executed, Peter was asleep, double-chained between two soldiers, with others standing guard before the prison gate, when suddenly there was a light in the cell and an angel of the Lord stood beside Peter! The angel slapped him on the side to awaken him and said, "Quick! Get up!" And the chains fell off his wrists! Then the angel told him, "Get dressed and put on your shoes." And he did. "Now put on your coat and follow me!" the angel ordered.

So Peter left the cell and followed the angel. But all the time he thought it was a dream or vision and didn't believe it was really happening. They passed the first and second cellblocks

and came to the iron gate of the street, which opened to them of its own accord! So they passed through and walked along together for a block, and then the angel left him.

Peter finally realized what had happened! "It's really true!" he said to himself. "The Lord has sent his angel and saved me from Herod and from what the Jews were hoping to do to me!" After a little thought, he went to the home of Mary, mother of John Mark, where many were gathered for a prayer meeting.

He knocked at the door in the gate, and a girl named Rhoda came to open it. When she recognized Peter's voice, she was so overjoyed that she ran back inside to tell everyone that Peter was standing outside in the street. They didn't believe her. "You're out of your mind," they said. When she insisted, they decided, "It must be his angel. They must have killed him."

Meanwhile Peter continued knocking. When they finally went out and opened the door, their surprise knew no bounds. He motioned for them to quiet down and told them what had happened and how the Lord had brought him out of jail. "Tell James and the others what happened," he said—and left for safer quarters.

At dawn, the jail was in great commotion. What had happened to Peter? When Herod sent for him and found that he wasn't there, he had the sixteen guards arrested, court-martialed, and sentenced to death. Afterward he left to live in Caesaria for a while.

While he was in Caesarea, a delegation from Tyre and Sidon arrived to see him. He was highly displeased with the people of those two cities, but the delegates made friends with Blastus, the royal secretary, and asked for peace, for their cities were economically dependent upon trade with Herod's country. An appointment with Herod was granted, and when the day arrived, he put on his royal robes, sat on his throne, and made a speech to them. At its conclusion the people gave him a great ovation, shouting, "It is the voice of a god and not of a man!"

Instantly, an angel of the Lord struck Herod with a sickness such that he was filled with maggots and died—because he accepted the people's worship instead of giving the glory to God.

God's good news was spreading rapidly, and there were many new believers.

Barnabas and Paul now visited Jerusalem and, as soon as they had finished their business, returned to Antioch, taking John Mark with them.

'A Light to the Gentiles'

AMONG THE PROPHETS and teachers of the church at Antioch were Barnabas and Symeon (also called the Black Man), Lucius (from Cyrene), Manaen (the foster-brother of King Herod), and Paul. One day as these men were worshiping and fasting, the Holy Spirit said, "Set apart Barnabas and Paul for a special job I have for them." So after more fasting and prayer, the men laid their hands on them—and sent them on their way.

Directed by the Holy Spirit, they went to Seleucia and then sailed for Cyprus. There, in the town of Salamis, they went to the Jewish synagogue and preached. (John Mark went with them as their assistant.)

Afterward they preached from town to town across the entire island until, finally, they reached Paphos, where they met a Jewish sorcerer, a fake prophet named Bar-Jesus. He had attached himself to the governor, Sergius Paulus, a man of considerable insight and understanding. The governor invited Barnabas and Paul to visit him, for he wanted to hear their message from God. But Elymas (his name means "the sorcerer" in Greek) interfered and urged the governor to pay no attention to

42

what Paul and Barnabas said, trying to keep him from trusting the Lord.

Then Paul, filled with the Holy Spirit, glared angrily at the sorcerer and said: "You son of the devil, full of every sort of trickery and villainy, enemy of all that is good, will you never end your opposition to the Lord? And now God has laid his hand of punishment upon you, and you will be stricken awhile with blindness."

Instantly mist and darkness fell upon him, and he began wandering around, begging for someone to take his hand and lead him. When the governor saw what happened, he believed and was astonished at the power of God's message.

Now Paul and those with him left Paphos by ship for Turkey, landing at the port town of Perga. There John deserted them and returned to Jerusalem. But Barnabas and Paul went on to Antioch, a city in the province of Pisidia.

On the Sabbath, they went into the synagogue for the services. After the usual readings from the Books of Moses and from the prophets, those in charge of the service sent them this message: "Brothers, if you have any word of instruction for us, come and give it!"

So Paul stood, waved a greeting to them, and began. "Men of Israel," he said, "and all others here who reverence God, let me begin my remarks with a bit of history.

"The God of this nation Israel chose our ancestors and honored them in Egypt by gloriously leading them out of their slavery. And he nursed them through forty years of wandering around in the wilderness. Then he destroyed seven nations in Canaan and gave Israel their land as an inheritance. Judges ruled for about 430 years and were followed by Samuel the prophet.

"Then the people begged for a king, and God gave them Saul (son of Kish), a man of the tribe of Benjamin, who reigned for forty years. But God removed him and replaced him with David as king, about whom God said, 'David (son of Jesse) is a man after my own heart, for he will obey me.' And it is one of King David's descendants, Jesus, who is God's promised Savior of Israel!

"But before he came, John the Baptist preached the need for everyone in Israel to turn from sin to God. As John was finishing his work, he asked: 'Do you think I am the Messiah? No! But he is coming soon—and in comparison with him I am utterly worthless.'

"Brothers—you sons of Abraham, and also all of you gentiles here who reverence God—this salvation is for all of us! The Jews in Jerusalem and their leaders fulfilled prophecy by killing Jesus; for they didn't recognize him or realize that he is the one the prophets had written about, though they heard the prophets' words read every Sabbath. They found no just cause to execute him but asked Pilate to have him killed anyway. When they had fulfilled all the prophecies concerning his death, he was taken from the cross and placed in a tomb.

"But God brought him back to life again! And he was seen many times during the next few days by the men who had accompanied him to Jerusalem from Galilee—these men have constantly testified to this in public witness.

"And now Barnabas and I are here to bring you this good news—that God's promise to our ancestors has come true in our own time, in that God brought Jesus back to life again. This is what the second psalm is talking about when it says concerning Jesus, 'Today I have honored you as my son.'

"For God had promised to bring him back to life again, no more to die. This is stated in the Scripture that says, 'I will do for you the wonderful thing I promised David.' In another psalm, he explained more fully, saying, 'God will not let his Holy One decay.' This was not a reference to David, for after David had served his generation according to the will of God, he died and was buried, and his body decayed. No, it was a reference to another—someone God brought back to life, whose body was not touched at all by the ravages of death.

44

"Brothers! Listen! In this man Jesus, there is forgiveness for your sins! Everyone who trusts in him is freed from all guilt and declared righteous—something the Jewish law could never do. Oh, be careful! Don't let the prophets' words apply to you. For they said, 'Look and perish, you despisers of the truth, for I am doing something in your day—something that you won't believe when you hear it announced.' "

As the people left the synagogue that day, they asked Paul to return and speak to them again the next week. And many Jews and godly gentiles who worshiped at the synagogue followed Paul and Barnabas down the street as the two men urged them to accept the mercies God was offering. The following week, almost the entire city turned out to hear them preach the word of God.

But when the Jewish leaders saw the crowds, they were jealous, and they cursed and argued against whatever Paul said.

Then Paul and Barnabas spoke out boldly and declared: "It was necessary that this good news from God should be given first to you Jews. But since you have rejected it and shown yourself unworthy of eternal life—well, we will offer it to gentiles. For this is as the Lord commanded when he said, 'I have made you a light to the gentiles, to lead them from the farthest corners of the earth to my salvation.' "

When the gentiles heard this, they were very glad and rejoiced in Paul's message; and as many as wanted eternal life believed. So God's message spread all through that region. Then the Jewish leaders stirred up both the godly women and the civic leaders of the city and incited a mob against Paul and Barnabas and ran them out of town. But they shook off the dust of their feet against the town and went on to the city of Iconium. And their converts were filled with joy and with the Holy Spirit.

CHAPTER FOURTEEN

Preaching on the Run

AT ICONIUM Paul and Barnabas went together to the synagogue and preached with such power that many—both Jews and gentiles—believed.

But the Jews who spurned God's message stirred up distrust among the gentiles against Paul and Barnabas, saying all sorts of evil things about them. Nevertheless, they stayed there a long time, preaching boldly, and the Lord proved their message was from him by giving them power to do great miracles. But the people of the city were divided in their opinion about them. Some agreed with the Jewish leaders, and some backed the apostles.

When Paul and Barnabas learned of a plot to incite a mob of gentiles, Jews, and Jewish leaders to attack and stone them, they fled for their lives, going to the cities of Lycaonia, Lystra, Derbe, and the surrounding area, and preaching the good news there.

While they were at Lystra, they came upon a man with crippled feet who had been that way from birth, so he had never walked. He was listening as Paul preached, and Paul noticed him and realized he had faith enough to be healed. So Paul called to him, "Stand up!" And the man leaped to his feet and started walking!

When the listening crowd saw what Paul had done, they shouted (in their local dialect, of course), "These men are gods in human bodies!" They decided that Barnabas was the Greek god Jupiter, and that Paul, because he was the chief speaker, was Mercury! The local priest of the Temple of Jupiter, located on the outskirts of the city, brought them cartloads of flowers and prepared to sacrifice oxen to them at the city gates before the crowds.

But when Barnabas and Paul saw what was happening, they ripped at their clothing in dismay and ran out among the people, shouting: "Men! What are you doing? We are merely human beings like yourselves! We have come to bring you the good news that you are invited to turn from the worship of these foolish things and to pray instead to the living God who made heaven and earth and sea and everything in them. In bygone days he permitted the nations to go their own ways, but he never left himself without a witness; there were always his reminders—the kind things he did, such as sending you rain and good crops and giving you food and gladness."

But even so, Paul and Barnabas could scarcely restrain the people from sacrificing to them!

Yet only a few days later, some Jews arrived from Antioch and Iconium and turned the crowds into a murderous mob that stoned Paul and dragged him out of the city, apparently dead. But as the believers stood around him, he got up and went back into the city!

The next day he left with Barnabas for Derbe. After preaching the good news there and making many disciples, they returned again to Lystra, Iconium, and Antioch, where they helped the believers to grow in love for God and each other. They encouraged them to continue in the faith in spite of all the persecution, reminding them that they must enter into the

Kingdom of God through many tribulations. Paul and Barnabas also appointed elders in every church and prayed for them with fasting, turning them over to the care of the Lord, in whom they trusted.

Then they traveled back through Pisidia to Pamphylia, preached again in Perga, and went on to Attalia.

Finally they returned by ship to Antioch, where their journey had begun, and where they had been committed to God for the work that was now completed.

Upon arrival, they called together the believers and reported on their trip, telling how God had opened the door of faith to the gentiles too. And they stayed there with the believers at Antioch for a long while.

Dissension and Decision

WHILE PAUL AND BARNABAS were at Antioch, some men from Judea arrived and began to teach the believers that unless they adhered to the ancient Jewish custom of circumcision, they could not be saved. Paul and Barnabas argued and discussed this with them at length, and finally the believers sent them to Jerusalem, accompanied by some local men, to talk to the apostles and elders there about this question. After the entire congregation had escorted them out of the city, the delegates went on to Jerusalem, stopping along the way in the cities of Phoenicia and Samaria to visit the believers, telling them—much to everyone's joy—that the gentiles, too, were being converted.

Arriving in Jerusalem, they met with the church leaders—all the apostles and elders were present—and Paul and Barnabas reported on what God had been doing through their ministry. But then some of the men who had been Pharisees before their conversion stood to their feet and declared that all gentile converts must be circumcised and required to follow all the Jewish customs and ceremonies. So the apostles and church elders set a further meeting to decide this question.

At the meeting, after long discussion, Peter stood and addressed them as follows: "Brothers, you all know that God chose me from among you long ago to preach the good news to the gentiles so that they also might believe. God, who knows men's hearts, confirmed the fact that he accepts gentiles by giving them the Holy Spirit, just as he gave him to us. He made no distinction between them and us, for he cleansed their lives through faith, just as he did ours. And now are you going to correct God by burdening the gentiles with a yoke that neither we nor our fathers were able to bear? Don't you believe that all are saved the same way, by the free gift of the Lord Jesus?"

There was no further discussion, and everyone now listened as Barnabas and Paul told about the miracles God had done through them among the gentiles.

When they had finished, James took the floor. "Brothers," he said, "listen to me. Peter has told you about the time God first visited the gentiles to take from them a people to bring honor to his name. And this fact of gentile conversion agrees with what the prophets predicted. For instance, listen to these words of the Lord as spoken through the prophet Amos: 'Afterward, I will return and renew the broken contract with David so that gentiles, too, will find the Lord—all those marked with my name.' That is what the Lord says, who reveals his plans made from the beginning.

"And so my judgment is that we should not insist that the gentiles who turn to God must obey our Jewish laws, except that we should write to them to refrain from eating meat sacrificed to idols, from all fornication, and also from eating unbled meat of strangled animals. For these things have been preached against in Jewish synagogues in every city on every Sabbath for many generations."

Then the apostles and elders and the whole congregation voted to send delegates to Antioch with Paul and Barnabas to report on this decision. The men chosen were two of the church leaders—Judas (also called Barsabbas) and Silas. This is the letter they took along with them:

> FROM: The apostles, elders, and brothers at Jerusalem.
> TO: The gentile brothers in Antioch, Syria, and Cilicia. Greetings!
>
> We understand that some believers from here have upset you and questioned your salvation, but they had no such instructions from us. So it seemed wise to us, having unanimously agreed on our decision, to send to you these two official representatives, along with our beloved Barnabas and Paul. These men—Judas and Silas, who have risked their lives for the sake of our Lord Jesus Christ—will confirm orally what we have decided concerning your question.
>
> For it seemed good to the Holy Spirit and to us to lay no greater burden of Jewish law on you than to abstain from eating food offered to idols and from unbled meat of strangled animals, and, of course, from fornication. If you do this, it is enough. Farewell.

The four messengers went at once to Antioch, where they called a general meeting of the Christians and gave them the letter. And there was great joy throughout the church that day as they read it.

Then Judas and Silas, both being gifted speakers, preached long sermons to the believers, strengthening their faith. They stayed several days, and then Judas and Silas returned to Jerusalem, taking greetings and appreciation to those who had sent them. Paul and Barnabas stayed on at Antioch to assist several others who were preaching and teaching there.

Several days later, Paul suggested to Barnabas that they return again to Turkey and visit each city where they had preached before to see how the new converts were getting along. Barnabas agreed and wanted to take along John Mark.

But Paul didn't like that idea at all, since John had deserted them in Pamphylia. Their disagreement over this was so sharp that they separated. Barnabas took Mark with him and sailed for Cyprus, while Paul chose Silas and, with the blessing of the believers, left for Syria and Cilicia to encourage the churches there.

CHAPTER SIXTEEN

Earthquake

PAUL AND SILAS went first to Derbe and then on to Lystra, where they met Timothy, a believer whose mother was a Christian Jewess but whose father was a Greek. Timothy was well thought of by the brothers in Lystra and Iconium, so Paul asked him to join them on their journey. In deference to the Jews of the area, he circumcised Timothy before they left, for everyone knew that his father was a Greek and hadn't permitted this before. Then they went from city to city, making known the decision concerning the gentiles, as decided by the apostles and elders in Jerusalem. So the church grew in faith and numbers.

Next they traveled through Phrygia and Galatia because the Holy Spirit had told them not to go into the Turkish province of Ausia at that time. Then, going along the borders of Mysia, they headed north for the province of Bithynia, but again the Spirit of Jesus said no. So, instead, they went on through the province of Mysia to the city of Troas.

That night Paul had a vision. In his dream he saw a man over in Macedonia, Greece, pleading with him, "Come over here and help us." Well, that settled it. We would go to Macedonia, for we could only conclude that God was sending us to preach the good news there.

We went aboard a boat at Troas and sailed straight across to Samothrace and, the next day, on to Neapolis, finally reaching Philippi, a Roman colony just inside the Macedonian border, where we stayed several days.

On the Sabbath, we went a little way outside the city to a riverbank where, we understood, some people met for prayer, and we taught the Scriptures to some women who came. One of them was Lydia, a saleswoman from Thyatira, a merchant of purple cloth. She was already a worshiper of God, and as she listened to us, the Lord opened her heart and she accepted all that Paul was saying. She was baptized along with all her household and asked us to be her guests. "If you agree that I am faithful to the Lord," she said, "come and stay at my home." And she urged us until we did.

One day as we were going down to the place of prayer beside the river, we met a demon-possessed slave girl who was a fortune-teller and earned much money for her masters. She followed along behind us, shouting, "These men are servants of God, and they have come to tell you how to have your sins forgiven."

This went on day after day until Paul, in great distress, turned and spoke to the demon within her. "I command you in the name of Jesus Christ to come out of her," he said. And instantly it left her.

Her masters' hopes of wealth were now shattered; they grabbed Paul and Silas and dragged them before the judges at the marketplace.

"These Jews are corrupting our city," they shouted. "They are teaching the people to do things that are against the Roman laws."

A mob was quickly formed against Paul and Silas, and the judges ordered them stripped and beaten with wooden whips. Again and again the rods slashed down across their bared backs; and afterward they were thrown into prison. The jailer was threatened with death if they escaped. So, taking no chances, he put them in the inner dungeon and clamped their feet into the stocks.

Around midnight, as Paul and Silas were praying and singing hymns to the Lord—and the other prisoners were listening—suddenly there was a great earthquake; the prison was shaken to its foundations, all the doors flew open, and the chains of every prisoner fell off! The jailer wakened to see the prison doors wide open, and, assuming the prisoners had escaped, he drew his sword to kill himself.

But Paul yelled to him, "Don't do it! We are all here!"

Trembling with fear, the jailer called for lights and ran to the dungeon, where he flung himself down before Paul and Silas. He brought them out and begged them, "Sirs, what must I do to be saved?"

They replied, "Believe in the Lord Jesus and you will be saved, and your entire household."

Then they told him and all his household the good news from the Lord. That same hour, he washed their stripes and he and all his family were baptized. Then he brought them up into his house and set a meal before them. How he and his household rejoiced because all were now believers! The next morning the judges sent police officers over to tell the jailer, "Let those men go!" So the jailer told Paul they were free to leave.

But Paul replied: "Oh no they don't! They have publicly beaten us without trial and jailed us—and we are Roman citizens! So now they want us to leave secretly? Never! Let them come themselves and release us!"

The police officers reported to the judges, who feared for their lives when they heard Paul and Silas were Roman citizens. So they came to the jail and begged them to go, and brought them out and pled with them to leave the city. Paul and Silas then returned to the home of Lydia, where they met with the believers and preached to them once more before leaving town.

Idols at Athens

Now THEY TRAVELED through the cities of Amphipolis and Apollonia and came to Thessalonica, where there was a Jewish synagogue. As was Paul's custom, he went there to preach, and for three Sabbaths in a row he opened the Scriptures to the people, explaining the prophecies about the sufferings of the Messiah and his coming back to life, and proving that Jesus is the Messiah. Some who listened were persuaded and became converts—including a large number of godly Greek men, and also many important women of the city.

But the Jewish leaders were jealous and incited some worthless fellows from the streets to form a mob and start a riot. They attacked the home of Jason, planning to take Paul and Silas to the City Council for punishment.

Not finding them there, they dragged Jason and some of the other believers out and took them before the Council instead. "Paul and Silas have turned the rest of the world upside down, and now they are here disturbing our city," they shouted, "and Jason has let them into his home. They are all guilty of treason, for they claim another king, Jesus, instead of Caesar."

The people of the city, as well as the judges, were concerned at these reports and let them go only after they had posted bail.

That night the Christians hurried Paul and Silas to Berea, and, as usual, they went to the synagogue to preach. But the people of Berea were more open-minded than those in Thessalonica, and they gladly listened to the message. They searched the Scriptures day by day to check up on statements made by Paul and Silas to see if they were really so. As a result, many of them believed, including several prominent Greek women and many men also.

But when the Jews in Thessalonica learned that Paul was preaching in Berea, they went over and stirred up trouble. The believers acted at once, sending Paul on to the coast, while Silas and Timothy remained behind. Those accompanying Paul went on with him to Athens, then returned to Berea with a message for Silas and Timothy to hurry and join him.

While Paul was waiting for them in Athens, he was deeply troubled by the idols he saw everywhere in the city. He went to the synagogue for discussions with the Jews and the devout gentiles, and he spoke daily in the public square to all who happened to be there.

He also had an encounter with some of the Epicurean and Stoic philosophers. Their reaction when he told them about Jesus and his resurrection was: "He's a dreamer." Or: "He's pushing some foreign religion."

But they invited him to the forum at Mars Hill. "Come and tell us more about the new religion," they said, "for you are saying some rather startling things and we want to hear more." (I should explain that all the Athenians as well as the foreigners in Athens seem to spend all their time discussing the latest new ideas!)

So Paul, standing before them at the Mars Hill forum, addressed them as follows:

Men of Athens, I notice that you are very religious;
for as I was out walking, I saw your many altars, and

one of them had this inscription on it: TO THE UN-KNOWN GOD. You have been worshiping him without knowing who he is, and now I wish to tell you about him.

He made the world and everything in it, and since he is Lord of heaven and earth, he doesn't live in man-made temples; and human hands can't minister to his needs—for he has no needs! He himself gives life and breath to everything and satisfies every need there is. He created all the people of the world from one man, Adam, and scattered the nations across the face of the earth. He decided beforehand which should rise and fall, and when. He determined their boundaries.

His purpose in all of this is that they should seek after God, and by feeling their way toward him, find him—though he is not far from any one of us. For in him we live and move and are! As one of your own poets says it, "We are the sons of God." If this be true, we shouldn't think of God as an idol made by men from gold or silver or chipped from stone. God tolerated man's past ignorance about these things, but now he commands everyone to put away idols and worship only him. For he has set a day for justly judging the world by the man he has appointed; and he has pointed him out by bringing him back to life again.

When they heard Paul speak of the resurrection of a person who had been dead, some laughed, but others said, "We want to hear more about this later." That ended Paul's discussion with them, but a few joined him and became believers. Among them was Dionysius, a member of the City Council, and a woman named Damaris, and others.

CHAPTER EIGHTEEN

Accused by the Jews

THEN PAUL LEFT ATHENS and went to Corinth. There he became acquainted with a Jew named Aquila, born in Pontus, who had recently arrived from Italy with his wife, Priscilla. They had been expelled from Italy as a result of Claudius Caesar's order to deport all Jews from Rome. Paul lived and worked with them, for they were tentmakers, just as he was.

Each Sabbath found Paul at the synagogue, trying to convince the Jews and Greeks alike. And after the arrival of Silas and Timothy from Macedonia, Paul spent his full time preaching and testifying to the Jews that Jesus is the Messiah. But when the Jews opposed him and blasphemed and hurled abuse at Jesus, Paul shook the dust from his robe and said, "Your blood be upon your own heads—I am innocent! From now on I will preach to the gentiles."

After that he stayed with Titus Justus, a gentile who worshiped God and lived next door to the synagogue. However, Crispus, the leader of the synagogue, and all his household believed in the Lord and were baptized—as were many others in Corinth.

One night the Lord spoke to Paul in a vision and told him: "Don't be afraid! Speak out! Don't quit! For I am with you and no one can harm you. Many people here in this city belong to me." So Paul stayed there the next year and a half, teaching the truths of God.

But when Gallio became governor of Achaia, the Jews rose in concerted action against Paul and brought him before the governor for judgment. They accused Paul of "persuading men to worship God in ways that are contrary to Roman law." But just as Paul started to make his defense, Gallio turned to his accusers and said: "Listen, you Jews, if this were a case involving some crime, I would be obliged to listen to you, but since it is merely a bunch of questions of semantics and personalities and your silly Jewish laws, you take care of it. I'm not interested and I'm not touching it." And he drove them out of the courtroom.

Then the mob grabbed Sosthenes, the new leader of the synagogue, and beat him outside the courtroom. But Gallio couldn't have cared less.

Paul stayed in the city several days after that, then said goodbye to the Christians and sailed for the coast of Syria, taking Priscilla and Aquila with him. At Cenchreae, Paul had his head shaved according to Jewish custom, for he had taken a vow. Arriving at the port of Ephesus, he left us aboard ship while he went over to the synagogue for a discussion with the Jews. They asked him to stay for a few days, but he felt that he had no time to lose.

"I must by all means be at Jerusalem for the holiday," he said. But he promised to return to Ephesus later if God permitted, and so we set sail again.

The next stop was the port of Caesarea, from which he visited the church at Jerusalem and then sailed on to Antioch. After spending some time there, he left for Turkey again, going through Galatia and Phrygia, visiting all the believers, encouraging them, and helping them grow in the Lord.

As it happened, a Jew named Apollos, a wonderful Bible teacher and preacher, had just arrived in Ephesus from Alexandria in Egypt. While he was in Egypt, someone had told him about John the Baptist and what John had said about Jesus, but that is all he knew. He had never heard the rest of the story! So he was preaching boldly and enthusiastically in the synagogue, "The Messiah is coming! Get ready to receive him!" Priscilla and Aquila were there and heard him—and it was a powerful sermon. Afterward, they met with him and explained what had happened to Jesus since the time of John, and all that it meant!

Apollos had been thinking about going to Greece, and the believers encouraged him in this. They wrote to their fellow believers there, telling them to welcome him. And upon his arrival in Greece, he was greatly used by God to strengthen the church, for he powerfully refuted all the Jewish arguments in public debate, showing by the Scriptures that Jesus is indeed the Messiah.

The Tradesmen Riot

WHILE APOLLOS WAS IN CORINTH, Paul traveled through Turkey and arrived in Ephesus, where he found several disciples. "Did you receive the Holy Spirit when you believed?" he asked them.

"No," they replied, "we don't know what you mean. What is the Holy Spirit?"

"Then what beliefs did you acknowledge at your baptism?" he asked.

And they replied, "What John the Baptist taught."

Then Paul pointed out to them that John's baptism was to demonstrate a desire to turn from sin to God and that those receiving his baptism must then go on to believe in Jesus, the one John said would come later.

As soon as they heard this, they were baptized in the name of the Lord Jesus. Then, when Paul laid his hands on their heads, the Holy Spirit came upon them and they spoke in other languages and prophesied. The men involved were about twelve in number.

Then Paul went to the synagogue and preached boldly each

Sabbath day for three months, telling what he believed and why, and persuading many to believe in Jesus. But some rejected his message and publicly spoke against Christ, so he left, refusing to preach to them again. Pulling out the believers, he began a separate meeting at the lecture hall of Tyrannus, and preached there daily. This went on for the next two years, so that everyone in the Turkish province of Ausia—both Jews and Greeks—heard the Lord's message. And God gave Paul the power to do unusual miracles, so that even when his handkerchiefs or parts of his clothing were placed upon sick people, they were healed and any demons within them came out.

A team of itinerant Jews who were traveling from town to town casting out demons planned to experiment by using the name of the Lord Jesus. The incantation they decided on was this: "I adjure you by Jesus, whom Paul preaches, to come out!" Seven sons of Sceva, a Jewish priest, were doing this. But when they tried it on a man possessed by a demon, the demon replied, "I know Jesus and I know Paul, but who are you?" And he leaped on two of them and beat them until they fled from his house naked and badly injured.

The story of what happened spread quickly all through Ephesus, to Jews and Greeks alike; and a solemn fear descended on the city, and the name of the Lord Jesus was greatly honored. Many of the believers who had been practicing black magic confessed their deeds and brought their incantation books and charms and burned them at a public bonfire. (Someone estimated the value of the books at $10,000.) This indicates how deeply the whole area was stirred by God's message.

Afterward, Paul felt impelled by the Holy Spirit to go across to Greece before returning to Jerusalem. "And after that," he said, "I must go on to Rome!" He sent his two assistants, Timothy and Erastus, on ahead to Greece while he stayed a bit longer in Turkey.

But about that time, a big blowup was brewing in Ephesus concerning the Christians. It began with Demetrius, a silversmith who employed many craftsmen to manufacture silver shrines of the Greek goddess Diana. He called a meeting of his men, together with others employed in related trades, and addressed them as follows:

"Gentlemen, this business is our income. As you know so well from what you've seen and heard, this man Paul has persuaded many, many people that handmade gods aren't gods at all. As a result, our sales volume is going down! And this trend is evident not only here in Ephesus but throughout the entire province! Of course, I am not talking only about the business aspects of this situation and our loss of income but also about the possibility that the temple of the great goddess Diana will lose its influence and that Diana—this magnificent goddess worshiped not only throughout this part of Turkey but all around the world—will be forgotten!"

At this their anger boiled and they began shouting, "Great is Diana of the Ephesians!"

A crowd began to gather, and soon the city was filled with confusion. Everyone rushed to the amphitheater, dragging along Gaius and Aristarchus, Paul's traveling companions, for trial. Paul wanted to go in, but the disciples wouldn't let him. Some of the Roman officers of the province, friends of Paul, also sent a message to him, begging him not to risk his life by entering.

Inside, the people were all shouting, some one thing and some another—everything was in confusion. In fact, most of them didn't even know why they were there.

Alexander was spotted among the crowd by some of the Jews and dragged forward. He motioned for silence and tried to speak. But when the crowd realized he was a Jew, they started shouting again and kept it up for two hours: "Great is Diana of the Ephesians! Great is Diana of the Ephesians!"

At last the mayor was able to quiet them down enough to speak. "Men of Ephesus," he said, "everyone knows that Ephesus is the center of the religion of the great Diana, whose image fell down to us from heaven. Since this is an indisputable fact, you shouldn't be disturbed, no matter what is said, and you should do nothing rash. Yet you have brought these men here who have stolen nothing from her temple and have not defamed her. If Demetrius and the craftsmen have a case against them, the courts are currently in session and the judges can take the case at once. Let them go through legal channels. And if there are complaints about other matters, they can be settled at the regular City Council meetings; for we are in danger of being called to account by the Roman government for today's riot, since there is no cause for it. And if Rome demands an explanation, I won't know what to say."

Then he dismissed them, and they dispersed.

CHAPTER TWENTY

A Last Good-bye

WHEN IT WAS ALL OVER, Paul sent for the disciples, preached a farewell message to them, said good-bye, and left for Greece, preaching to the believers along the way in all the cities he passed through. He was in Greece three months, preparing to sail for Syria, when he discovered a plot by the Jews against his life, so he decided to go north to Macedonia first.

Several men were traveling with him, going as far as Turkey: Sopater of Berea, the son of Pyrrhus; Aristarchus and Secundus, from Thessalonica; Gaius, from Derbe; Timothy; and Tychicus and Trophimus, who were returning to their homes in Turkey and had gone on ahead and were waiting for us at Troas. As soon as the Passover ceremonies ended, we boarded ship at Philippi in northern Greece and five days later arrived in Troas, Turkey, where we stayed a week.

On Sunday, we gathered together to break bread, with Paul preaching. And since he was leaving the next day, he talked until midnight! The upstairs room where we met was lighted with many flickering lamps; and as Paul spoke on and on, a young man named Eutychus, who was sitting on the window-

67

sill, went fast asleep and fell three stories to his death. Paul went down and took him into his arms. "Don't worry," he said, "he's all right!" And he was! What a wave of awesome joy swept through the crowd! They all went back upstairs and ate the Lord's Supper together. Then Paul preached another long sermon—so it was dawn when he finally left them!

Paul was going by land to Assos, and we went on ahead by ship. He joined us there, and we sailed together to Mitylene; the next day we passed Chios; the next, we touched at Samos; and a day later we arrived at Miletus.

Paul had decided against stopping at Ephesus this time, as he was hurrying to get to Jerusalem, if possible, for the celebration of Pentecost. But when we landed at Miletus, he sent a message to the elders of the church at Ephesus, asking them to come down to the boat to meet him.

When they arrived, he told them: "You men know that from the day I set foot in Turkey until now, I have done the Lord's work humbly—yes, and with tears—and have faced grave danger from the plots of the Jews against my life. Yet I never shrank from telling you the truth, either publicly or in your homes. I have had one message for Jews and gentiles alike—the necessity of turning from sin to God through faith in our Lord Jesus Christ.

"And now I am going to Jerusalem, drawn there irresistibly by the Holy Spirit, not knowing what awaits me, except that the Holy Spirit has told me in city after city that jail and suffering lie ahead. But life is worth nothing unless I use it for doing the work assigned me by the Lord Jesus—the work of telling others the good news about God's mighty kindness and love.

"And now I know that none of you among whom I went about teaching the Kingdom will ever see me again. Let me say plainly that no man's blood can be laid at my door, for I didn't shrink from declaring all of God's message to you.

"And now, beware! Be sure that you feed and shepherd God's flock—his church, purchased with his blood—for the Holy Spirit is holding you responsible as overseers. I know full well that after I leave you, false teachers, like vicious wolves, will appear among you, not sparing the flock. Some of you yourselves will distort the truth in order to draw a following. Watch out! Remember the three years I was with you—my constant watchful concern over you night and day and the many tears I shed over you.

"And now I entrust you to God and his care and to his wonderful words, which are able to build your faith and give you all the inheritance of those who are set apart for himself.

"I have never been hungry for money or fine clothing—you know that these hands of mine worked to pay my own way and even to supply the needs of those who were with me. And I was a constant example to you in helping the poor; for I remembered the words of the Lord Jesus: 'It is more blessed to give than to receive.' "

When he had finished speaking, he knelt and prayed with them, and they wept aloud as they embraced him in farewell, sorrowing most of all because he said that he would never see them again. Then they accompanied him down to the ship.

CHAPTER TWENTY-ONE

Saved by Soldiers

AFTER PARTING from the Ephesian elders, we sailed straight to Cos. The next day we reached Rhodes and then went to Patara. There we boarded a ship sailing for the Syrian province of Phoenicia. We sighted the island of Cyprus, passed it on our left, and landed at the harbor of Tyre, in Syria, where the ship unloaded. We went ashore, found the local believers, and stayed with them a week. These disciples warned Paul—the Holy Spirit prophesying through them—not to go on to Jerusalem. At the end of the week, when we returned to the ship, the entire congregation, including wives and children, walked with us down to the beach, where we prayed and said our farewells. Then we went aboard and they returned home.

The next stop after leaving Tyre was Ptolemais, where we greeted the believers but stayed only one day. Then we went on to Caesarea and stayed at the home of Philip the Evangelist, one of the first seven deacons. He had four unmarried daughters who had the gift of prophecy.

During our stay of several days, a man named Agabus, who also had the gift of prophecy, arrived from Judea and visited us.

He took Paul's belt, bound his own feet and hands with it, and said, "The Holy Spirit declares, 'So shall the owner of this belt be bound by the Jews in Jerusalem and turned over to the Romans.'" Hearing this, all of us—the local believers and his traveling companions—begged Paul not to go on to Jerusalem.

But he said: "Why all this weeping? You are breaking my heart! For I am ready not only to be jailed at Jerusalem but also to die for the sake of the Lord Jesus." When it was clear that he wouldn't be dissuaded, we gave up and said, "The will of the Lord be done."

So, shortly afterward, we packed our things and left for Jerusalem. Some disciples from Caesarea accompanied us, and on arrival we were guests at the home of Mnason, originally from Cyprus, one of the early believers; and all the believers at Jerusalem welcomed us cordially.

The second day, Paul took us with him to meet with James and the elders of the Jerusalem church. After greetings were exchanged, Paul recounted the many things God had accomplished among the gentiles through his work.

They praised God but then said: "You know, dear brother, how many thousands of Jews have also believed, and they are all very insistent that Jewish believers must continue to follow the Jewish traditions and customs. Our Jewish Christians here at Jerusalem have been told that you are against the laws of Moses, against our Jewish customs, and that you forbid the circumcision of their children. Now what can be done? For they will certainly hear that you have come.

"We suggest this: We have four men here who are preparing to shave their heads and take some vows. Go with them to the Temple and have your head shaved too—and pay for theirs to be shaved.

"Then everyone will know that you approve of this custom for the Hebrew Christians and that you yourself obey the Jewish laws and are in line with our thinking in these matters.

"As for the gentile Christians, we aren't asking them to fol-

low these Jewish customs at all—except for the ones we wrote to them about: not to eat food offered to idols, not to eat unbled meat from strangled animals, and not to commit fornication."

So Paul agreed to their request and, the next day, went with the men to the Temple for the ceremony, thus publicizing his vow to offer a sacrifice seven days later with the others.

The seven days were almost ended when some Jews from Turkey saw him in the Temple and roused a mob against him. They grabbed him, yelling: "Men of Israel! Help! Help! This is the man who preaches against our people and tells everybody to disobey the Jewish laws. He even talks against the Temple and defiles it by bringing gentiles in!" (For down in the city, earlier that day, they had seen him with Trophimus, a gentile from Ephesus in Turkey, and assumed that Paul had taken him into the Temple.)

The whole population of the city was electrified by these accusations, and a great riot followed. Paul was dragged out of the Temple, and immediately the gates were closed behind him. As they were about to kill him, word reached the commander of the Roman garrison that all Jerusalem was in an uproar. He quickly ordered out his soldiers and officers and ran down among the crowd. When the mob saw the troops coming, they quit beating Paul. The commander arrested him and ordered him bound with double chains. Then the commander asked the crowd who he was and what he had done. Some shouted one thing and some another. When he couldn't find out anything in all the uproar and confusion, he ordered Paul to be taken to the armory. As they reached the stairs, the mob grew so violent that the soldiers lifted Paul to their shoulders to protect him, and the crowd surged behind, shouting, "Away with him, away with him!"

As Paul was about to be taken inside, he said to the commander, "May I have a word with you?"

"Do you know Greek?" the commander asked, surprised. "Aren't you that Egyptian who led a rebellion a few years ago and took 4,000 members of the Assassins with him into the desert?''

''No,'' Paul replied, ''I am a Jew from Tarsus in Cilicia, which is no small town. I request permission to talk to these people.''

The commander agreed, so Paul stood on the stairs and motioned to the people to be quiet; soon a deep silence enveloped the crowd, and he began to speak to them in Hebrew.

CHAPTER TWENTY-TWO

Paul Tells His Story

Brothers and Fathers, listen to me as I offer my defense." (When they heard Paul speaking in Hebrew, the silence was even greater.) "I am a Jew," he said, "born in Tarsus, a city in Cilicia, but educated here in Jerusalem under Gamaliel, at whose feet I learned to follow our Jewish laws and customs very carefully. I became very anxious to honor God in everything I did, just as you have tried to do today. And I persecuted the Christians, hounding them to death, binding and delivering to prison both men and women. The High Priest or any member of the Council can testify that this is so. For I asked them for letters to the Jewish leaders in Damascus, with instructions to let me bring any Christians I found to Jerusalem in chains to be punished.

"As I was on the road, nearing Damascus, suddenly about noon a very bright light from heaven blazed around me. And I fell to the ground and heard a voice saying to me, 'Saul, Saul, why are you persecuting me?'

" 'Who is it speaking to me, sir?' I asked. And he replied, 'I am Jesus of Nazareth, the one you are persecuting.' The men with me saw the light but didn't hear what was said. And I said, 'What shall I do, Lord?'

"And the Lord told me, 'Get up and go into Damascus, and there you will be told what awaits you in the years ahead.'

"I was blinded by the intense light and had to be led into Damascus by my companions. There a man named Ananias, as godly a man as you could find for obeying the law, and well thought of by all the Jews of Damascus, came to me and, standing beside me, said, 'Brother Saul, receive your sight!'" And that very hour I could see him!

"Then he told me: 'The God of our fathers has chosen you to know his will and to see the Messiah and hear him speak. You are to take his message everywhere, telling what you have seen and heard. And now, why delay? Go and be baptized, and be cleansed from your sins, calling on the name of the Lord.'

"One day, after my return to Jerusalem, while I was praying in the Temple, I fell into a trance and saw a vision of God saying to me, 'Hurry! Leave Jerusalem, for the people here won't believe you when you give them my message.'

" 'But Lord,' I argued, 'they certainly know that I imprisoned and beat those in every synagogue who believed in you. And when your witness Stephen was killed, I was standing there agreeing—keeping the coats they laid aside as they stoned him.'

"But God said to me, 'Leave Jerusalem, for I will send you far away to the *gentiles!*' "

The crowd listened until Paul came to the word, then with one voice they shouted: "Away with such a fellow! Kill him! He isn't fit to live!" They yelled and threw their coats in the air and tossed up handfuls of dust.

So the commander brought him inside and ordered him lashed with whips to make him confess his crime. He wanted to find out why the crowd had become so furious!

As they tied Paul down to lash him, Paul said to an officer standing there, "Is it legal for you to whip a Roman citizen who hasn't even been tried?"

The officer went to the commander and asked, "What are you doing? This man is a Roman citizen!"

So the commander went over and asked Paul, "Tell me, are you a Roman citizen?"

"Yes, I certainly am."

"I am too," the commander muttered, "and it cost me plenty!"

"But I am a citizen by birth!"

The soldiers who were standing ready to lash him quickly disappeared when they heard that Paul was a Roman citizen, and the commander was frightened because he had ordered him bound and whipped

The next day, the commander freed him from his chains and ordered the chief priests into session with the Jewish Council. He had Paul brought in before them to try to find out what the trouble was all about.

CHAPTER TWENTY-THREE

The Plot to Kill Paul

GAZING INTENTLY at the Council, Paul began by saying, "Brothers, I have always lived before God in all good conscience!"

Instantly, Ananias the High Priest commanded those close to Paul to slap him on the mouth.

Paul said to him: "God shall slap you, you whitewashed pigpen. What kind of judge are you to break the law yourself by ordering me struck like that?"

Those standing near Paul said to him, "Is that the way to talk to God's High Priest?"

"I didn't realize he was the High Priest, brothers," Paul replied, "for the Scriptures say, 'Never speak evil of any of your rulers.' "

Then Paul thought of something! Some members of the Council were Sadducees, and some were Pharisees. So he shouted: "Brothers, I am a Pharisee, as were all my ancestors! And I am being tried here today because I believe in the resurrection of the dead!"

This divided the Council right down the middle—the

Pharisees against the Sadducees—for the Sadducees say there is no resurrection, nor angels, nor even an eternal spirit within us; but the Pharisees believe in all of these.

So a great clamor arose. Some of the Jewish leaders jumped up to argue that Paul was all right. "We see nothing wrong with him," they shouted. "Perhaps a spirit or angel spoke to him there on the Damascus road."

The shouting grew louder and louder, and the men were tugging at Paul from both sides, pulling him this way and that. Finally the commander, fearing they would tear him apart, ordered his soldiers to take Paul away from them by force and bring him back to the armory.

That night the Lord stood beside Paul and said, "Don't worry, Paul; just as you have told the people about me here in Jerusalem, so you must also in Rome."

The next morning some forty or more of the Jews got together and bound themselves by a curse neither to eat nor drink until they had killed Paul! Then they went to the chief priests and elders and told them what they had done. "Ask the commander to bring Paul back to the Council again," they requested. "Pretend you want to ask a few more questions. We will kill him on the way."

But Paul's nephew got wind of their plan and came to the armory and told Paul.

Paul called one of the officers and said: "Take this boy to the commander. He has something important to tell him."

So the officer did, explaining, "Paul, the prisoner, called me over and asked me to bring this young man to you to tell you something."

The commander took the boy by the hand and, leading him aside, asked, "What is it you want to tell me, lad?"

"Tomorrow," he told him, "the Jews are going to ask you to bring Paul before the Council again, pretending they want to get some more information. But don't do it! There are more than forty men hiding along the road, ready to jump him and kill him. They have bound themselves under a curse neither to eat nor drink till he is dead. They are out there now, expecting you to agree to their request."

"Don't let a soul know you told me this," the commander warned the boy as he left. Then the commander called two of his officers and ordered: "Get 200 soldiers ready to leave for Caesarea at nine o'clock tonight! Take 200 spearmen and 70 mounted cavalry. Give Paul a horse to ride, and get him safely to Governor Felix."

Then he wrote this letter to the governor:

FROM: Claudius Lysias
TO: His Excellency, Governor Felix. Greetings!

This man was seized by the Jews, who were about to kill him. So I sent the soldiers to rescue him, for I learned that he was a Roman citizen. Then I took him to their Council to try to find out what he had done. I soon discovered that it was something about their Jewish beliefs, certainly nothing worthy of imprisonment or death. But when I was informed of a plot to kill him, I decided to send him on to you, and I will tell his accusers to bring their charges before you.

So that night, as ordered, the soldiers took Paul to Antipatris. They returned to the armory the next morning, leaving him with the cavalry to take him on to Caesarea.

When they arrived in Caesarea, they presented Paul and the letter to the governor. He read it and then asked Paul where he was from.

"Cilicia," Paul answered.

"I will hear your case fully when your accusers arrive," the governor told him. Then he ordered Paul kept in the prison at King Herod's palace.

CHAPTER TWENTY-FOUR

Two Years in Prison

FIVE DAYS LATER, Ananias the High Priest arrived with some of the Jewish leaders and the lawyer Tertullus to make their accusations against Paul. When Tertullus was called forward, he laid charges against Paul in the following address to the governor:

"Your Excellency, you have given quietness and peace to us Jews and have greatly reduced the discrimination against us. And for this we are very, very grateful to you. But lest I bore you, kindly give me your attention for only a moment as I briefly outline our case against this man. We have found him to be a troublemaker, a man who is constantly inciting the Jews throughout the entire world to riots and rebellions against the Roman government. He is a ringleader of the sect known as the Nazarenes. Moreover, he was trying to defile the Temple when we arrested him.

"We would have given him what he justly deserves, but Lysias, the commander of the garrison, came and violently took him away from us, demanding that he be tried by Roman law. You can find out the truth of our accusations by examining the man yourself."

Then all the other Jews chimed in, declaring that everything Tertullus said was true.

Now it was Paul's turn. The governor motioned for him to rise and speak.

"I know, sir," Paul began, "that you have been a judge of Jewish affairs for many years, and this gives me confidence as I make my defense. You can quickly discover that it was no more than twelve days ago that I arrived in Jerusalem to worship at the Temple, and you will discover that I have never incited a riot in any synagogue or on the streets of any city; and these men certainly cannot prove the things they accuse me of doing.

"But one thing I do confess: that I believe in the way of salvation which they refer to as the Nazarene sect; I follow that system of serving the God of our ancestors; I firmly believe in the Jewish law and everything written in the books of prophecy, and I believe, just as these men do, that there will be a resurrection of both the righteous and the ungodly. Because of this, I try with all my strength always to maintain a clean conscience before God and man.

"After several years away, I returned to Jerusalem with money to aid the Jews and to offer a sacrifice to God. My accusers saw me in the Temple as I was presenting my thank offering. I had shaved my head, as their laws require, and there was no crowd around me, and no rioting! But some Jews from Turkey were there (who ought to be here if they have anything against me). But look! Ask these men right here what wrongdoing their Council found in me, except that I said one thing I shouldn't have when I shouted out, 'I am here before the Council to defend myself for believing that the dead will rise again!' "

Felix, who knew Christians don't go around starting riots, told the Jews to wait for the arrival of Lysias, the garrison commander, and then he would decide the case. He ordered Paul to prison but instructed the guards to treat him gently and not to forbid any of his friends from visiting him or bringing him gifts to make his stay more comfortable.

A few days later, Felix came to the prison with Drusilla, his legal wife, a Jewess. Sending for Paul, they listened as he told them about faith in Christ Jesus. And as he reasoned with them about righteousness and self-control and the judgment to come, Felix was terrified.

"Go away for now," he replied, "and when it is more convenient, I'll call for you again."

He also hoped that Paul would bribe him, so he sent for him from time to time and talked with him. Two years went by in this way; then Felix was succeeded by Porcius Festus. And because Felix wanted to gain favor with the Jews, he left Paul in chains.

CHAPTER TWENTY-FIVE

Paul Appeals to Caesar

T HREE DAYS AFTER FESTUS ARRIVED in Caesarea to take over his new responsibilities, he left for Jerusalem, where the chief priests and other Jewish leaders got hold of him and gave him their story about Paul. They begged him to bring Paul to Jerusalem at once. (Their plan was to waylay and kill him.) But Festus replied that since Paul was at Caesarea and he himself was returning there soon, those with authority in this affair should return with him for the trial.

Eight or ten days later, he returned to Caesarea and, the following day, opened Paul's trial.

On Paul's arrival in court, the Jews from Jerusalem gathered around, hurling many serious accusations that they couldn't prove. Paul denied the charges: "I am not guilty," he said. "I have not opposed the Jewish laws or desecrated the Temple or rebelled against the Roman government."

Then Festus, anxious to please the Jews, asked him, "Are you willing to go to Jerusalem and stand trial before me?"

But Paul replied, "No! I demand my privilege of a hearing before the Emperor himself. You know very well I am not guilty. I don't refuse to die! But if I am innocent, neither you nor anyone else has a right to turn me over to these men to kill me. *I appeal to Caesar.*"

Festus conferred with his advisers and then replied, "Very well! You have appealed to Caesar, and to Caesar you shall go!"

A few days later, King Agrippa arrived with Bernice, his sister, for a visit with Festus. During their stay of several days, Festus discussed Paul's case with the king. "There is a prisoner here," he told him, "whose case was left for me by Felix. When I was in Jerusalem, the chief priests and other Jewish leaders gave me their side of the story and asked me to have him killed. Of course, I quickly pointed out to them that Roman law does not convict a man before he is tried. He is given an opportunity to defend himself face-to-face with his accusers.

"When they came here for the trial, I called the case the very next day and ordered Paul brought in. But the accusations made against him weren't at all what I supposed they would be. It was something about their religion and about someone called Jesus, who died, but who Paul insists is alive! I was perplexed as to how to decide a case of this kind and asked him whether he would be willing to stand trial on these charges in Jerusalem. But Paul appealed to Caesar! So I ordered him back to jail until I could arrange to get him to the Emperor."

"I'd like to hear the man myself," Agrippa said.

And Festus replied, "You shall—tomorrow!"

So the next day, after the king and Bernice had arrived at the courtroom with great pomp, accompanied by military officers and prominent men of the city, Festus ordered Paul brought in.

Then Festus addressed the audience. "King Agrippa and all present," he said, "this is the man whose death is demanded both by the local Jews and by those in Jerusalem! But in my opinion he has done nothing worthy of death. However, he appealed his case to Caesar, and I have no alternative but to send him. But what shall I write the emperor? For there is no real charge against him! So I have brought him before you all, and especially you, King Agrippa, to examine him and then tell me what to write. For it doesn't seem reasonable to send a prisoner to the Emperor without any charges against him!"

Before King Agrippa

Then AGRIPPA SAID TO PAUL, "Go ahead, tell us your story."

So Paul, with many gestures, presented his defense:

"I am fortunate, King Agrippa," he began, "to be able to present my answer before you, for I know you are an expert on Jewish laws and customs. Now please listen patiently!

"As the Jews are well aware, I was given a thorough Jewish training from my earliest childhood in Tarsus, and later at Jerusalem, and I lived accordingly. If they would admit it, they know that I have always been the strictest of Pharisees when it comes to obedience to Jewish laws and customs. But the real reason behind their accusations is something else—it is because I am looking forward to the fulfillment of God's promise made to our ancestors. The twelve tribes of Israel strive night and day to attain the same hope I have! Yet, O King, for me it is a crime, they say! But is it a crime to believe in the resurrection of the dead? Does it seem incredible to you that God can bring men back to life again?

"I used to believe that I ought to do many horrible things to the followers of Jesus of Nazareth. I imprisoned many of the saints in Jerusalem, as authorized by the High Priests; and when they faced the death penalty, I cast my vote against them. I used torture to try to make Christians everywhere curse Christ. I was so violently opposed to them that I hounded them even in distant cities in foreign lands.

"I was on such a mission to Damascus, armed with the authority and commission of the chief priests when, one day about noon, sir, a light from heaven brighter than the sun shone down on me and my companions. We all fell down, and I heard a voice speaking to me in Hebrew: 'Saul, Saul, why are you persecuting me? You are only hurting yourself.'

" 'Who are you, sir?' I asked.

"And the Lord replied: 'I am Jesus, the one you are persecuting. Now stand up! For I have appeared to you to appoint you as my servant and my witness. You are to tell the world about this experience and about the many other occasions when I shall appear to you. And I will protect you from both your own people and the gentiles. Yes, I am going to send you to the gentiles to open their eyes to their true condition so that they may repent and live in the light of God instead of in Satan's darkness; so that they may receive forgiveness for their sins and God's inheritance along with all people everywhere whose sins are cleansed away, who are set apart by faith in me.'

"And so, O King Agrippa, I was not disobedient to that vision from heaven! I preached first to those in Damascus, then in Jerusalem and through Judea, and also to the gentiles, that all must forsake their sins and turn to God—and prove their repentance by doing good deeds. The Jews arrested me in the Temple for preaching this and tried to kill me, but God protected me so that I am still alive today to tell these facts to everyone, both great and small. I teach nothing except what the prophets and Moses said— that the Messiah would suffer and be the first to rise from the dead to bring light to Jews and gentiles alike."

Suddenly Festus shouted: "Paul, you are insane. Your long studying has broken your mind!"

But Paul replied: "I am not insane, Most Excellent Festus. I speak words of sober truth. And King Agrippa knows about these things. I speak frankly, for I am sure these events are all familiar to him, since they were not done in a corner! King Agrippa, do you believe the prophets? But I know you do —"

Agrippa interrupted him. "With trivial proofs like these, you expect me to become a Christian?"

And Paul replied, "Would to God that whether my arguments are trivial or strong, both you and everyone here in this audience might become the same as I am—except for these chains."

Then the king, the governor, Bernice, and all the others stood. As they talked it over afterward, they agreed: "This man hasn't done anything worthy of death or imprisonment."

And Agrippa said to Festus, "He could be set free if he hadn't appealed to Caesar!"

CHAPTER TWENTY-SEVEN

Shipwreck

ARRANGEMENTS WERE FINALLY MADE to start us on our way to Rome by ship, so Paul and several other prisoners were placed in the custody of an officer named Julius, a member of the imperial guard. We left on a boat that was scheduled to make several stops along the Turkish coast. I should add that Aristarchus, a Greek from Thessalonica, was with us.

The next day, when we docked at Sidon, Julius was very kind to Paul and let him go ashore to visit with friends and receive their hospitality. Putting to sea from there, we encountered headwinds that made it difficult to keep the ship on course, so we sailed north of Cyprus, between the island and the mainland, and passed along the coast of the provinces of Cilicia and Pamphylia, landing at Myra, in the province of Lycia. There our officer found an Egyptian ship from Alexandria that was bound for Italy and put us aboard.

After several days of rough sailing, we finally neared Cnidus; but the winds had become too strong, so we ran across to Crete, passing the port of Salmone. Beating into the wind with great difficulty and moving slowly along the southern coast, we arrived at Fair Havens, near the city of Lasea. There we stayed for several days. The weather was becoming dangerous for long voyages by then, since it was late in the year, and Paul spoke to the ship's officers about it.

"Sirs," he said, "I believe there is trouble ahead if we go on—perhaps shipwreck, loss of cargo, injuries, and death." But the officers in charge of the prisoners listened more to the ship's captain and the owner than to Paul. And since Fair Havens was an exposed harbor—a poor place to spend the winter—most of the crew advised trying to go farther up the coast to Phoenix in order to winter there; Phoenix was a good harbor, with only a northwest and southwest exposure.

Just then a light wind began blowing from the south, and it looked like a perfect day for the trip; so they pulled up anchor and sailed along close to shore.

But shortly afterward, the weather changed abruptly, and a heavy wind of typhoon strength (a "northeaster," they called it) caught the ship and blew it out to sea. They tried at first to face back to shore but couldn't, so they gave up and let the ship run before the gale.

We finally sailed behind a small island named Clauda, where with great difficulty we hoisted aboard the lifeboat that was being towed behind us, then banded the ship with ropes to strengthen the hull. The sailors were afraid of being driven across to the quicksands of the African coast, so they lowered the topsails and were thus driven before the wind.

The next day, as the seas grew higher, the crew began throwing the cargo overboard. The following day they threw out the tackle and anything else they could lay their hands on. The terrible storm raged unabated for many days until, at last, all hope was gone.

No one had eaten for a long time, but finally Paul called the crew together and said: "Men, you should have listened to me in the first place and not left Fair Havens—you would have avoided all this injury and loss! But cheer up! Not one of us will lose his life, even though the ship will go down.

"For last night an angel of the God to whom I belong and whom I serve stood beside me and said: 'Don't be afraid, Paul—for you will surely stand trial before Caesar! What's more, God has granted your request and will save the lives of all those sailing with you.' So take courage! For I believe God! It will be just as he said! But we will be shipwrecked on an island."

About midnight on the fourteenth night of the storm, as we were being driven to and fro on the Adriatic Sea, the sailors suspected land was near. They sounded the bottom and found 120 feet of water below them. A little later they sounded again and found only 90 feet. At this rate, they knew they would soon be driven ashore, and, fearing rocks along the coast, they threw out four anchors from the stern and prayed for daylight.

Some of the sailors, planning to abandon the ship, lowered the emergency boat as though they were going to put out anchors from the prow. But Paul said to the soldiers and their commanding officer, "You will all die unless everyone stays aboard." So the soldiers cut the ropes and let the boat fall off.

As the darkness gave way to the early morning light, Paul begged everyone to eat. "You haven't touched food for two weeks," he said. "Please eat something now for your own good! For not a hair of your heads shall perish!"

Then he took some hardtack, gave thanks to God before them all, and broke off a piece and ate it. Suddenly everyone felt better and began eating, all 276 of us—for that is the number we had aboard. After eating, the crew lightened the ship further by throwing all the wheat overboard.

When it was day, they didn't recognize the coastline but noticed a bay with a beach and wondered whether they could get between the rocks and be driven up onto the beach. They finally decided to try. Cutting off the anchors and leaving them in the sea, they lowered the rudders, raised the foresail, and headed ashore. But the ship hit a sandbar and ran aground. The bow

of the ship stuck fast, while the stern was exposed to the violence of the waves and began to break apart.

The soldiers advised their commanding officer to let them kill the prisoners lest any of them swim ashore and escape. But Julius wanted to spare Paul, so he told them no. Then he ordered all who could swim to jump overboard and make for land, and the rest to try for it on planks and debris from the broken ship. So everyone escaped safely ashore!

Under House Arrest

W E SOON LEARNED that we were on the island of Malta. The people of the island were very kind to us, building a bonfire on the beach to welcome and warm us in the rain and cold.

As Paul gathered an armful of sticks to lay on the fire, a poisonous snake, driven out by the heat, fastened itself onto his hand! The people of the island saw it hanging there and said to each other: "A murderer, no doubt! Though he escaped the sea, justice will not permit him to live!"

But Paul shook off the snake into the fire and was unharmed. The people waited for him to begin swelling or suddenly fall dead; but when they had waited a long time and no harm came to him, they changed their minds and decided he was a god.

Near the shore where we landed was an estate belonging to Publius, the governor of the island. He welcomed us courteously and fed us for three days. As it happened, Publius' father was ill with fever and dysentery. Paul went in and prayed for him and, laying his hands on him, healed him! Then all the other sick people on the island came and were cured. As a result, we were showered with gifts, and when the time came to sail, people put on board all sorts of things we would need for the trip.

It was three months after the shipwreck before we set sail again, and this time it was in *The Twin Brothers*, of Alexandria, a ship that had wintered at the island. Our first stop was Syracuse, where we stayed three days. From there we circled around to Rhegium; a day later a south wind began blowing, so the following day we arrived at Puteoli, where we found some believers! They begged us to stay with them seven days. Then we went on to Rome.

The brothers in Rome had heard we were coming and came to meet us at the Forum on the Appian Way. Others joined us at the Three Taverns. When Paul saw them, he thanked God and took courage.

When we arrived in Rome, Paul was permitted to live wherever he wanted to, though he was guarded by a soldier. Three days after his arrival, he called together the local Jewish leaders and spoke to them.

"Brothers," he began, "I was arrested by the Jews in Jerusalem and handed over to the Roman government for prosecution, even though I had neither harmed anyone nor violated the customs of our ancestors. The Romans gave me a trial and wanted to release me, for they found no cause for the death sentence demanded by the Jewish leaders. But when the Jews protested the decision, I felt it necessary, with no malice against them, to appeal to Caesar. I asked you to come here today so we could get acquainted and I could tell you that it is because I believe the Messiah has come that I am bound with this chain."

They replied: "We have heard nothing against you! We have had no letters from Judea or reports from those arriving from Jerusalem. But we want to hear what you believe, for the only thing we know about these Christians is that they are denounced everywhere!"

So a time was set, and on that day large numbers came to his house. He told them about the Kingdom of God and taught them about Jesus from the Scriptures—from the five books of Moses and the books of prophecy. He began lecturing in the morning and went on into the evening!

Some believed and some didn't. But after they had argued back and forth among themselves, they left with this final word from Paul ringing in their ears: "The Holy Spirit was right when he said through Isaiah the prophet: 'Say to the Jews, "You will hear and see but not understand, for your hearts are too fat and your ears don't listen and you have closed your eyes against understanding, for you don't want to see and hear and understand and turn to me to heal you." ' So I want you to realize that this salvation from God is available to the gentiles, too, and they will accept it."

Paul lived for the next two years in his rented house and welcomed all who visited him, telling them with all boldness about the Kingdom of God and about the Lord Jesus Christ; and no one tried to stop him.

Luke does not tell us the outcome of Paul's trial. Tradition and the weight of historical evidence agree that he was acquitted and released, probably about 63 A.D. The remaining years of his life were spent carrying the good news of salvation to Greece and Asia Minor and, perhaps, elsewhere. During the persecution of the church under the emperor Nero, Paul was once again arrested, brought back to Rome, and put to death in 67 A.D. Tertullian, a second-century historian, says that he was beheaded. On the same day, Peter was martyred by being crucified—upside down.

About the Author

LUKE, WHO WAS GREEK BY BIRTH, wrote in the Greek language for Greek-speaking readers. He was well educated—Paul refers to him as "the beloved physician"—and an early convert to Christianity.

In about the year 63, Luke wrote his Gospel. It has been called "the most beautiful book ever written," yet Luke did not himself witness the events he speaks of.

Soon after, Luke wrote a second book, telling of events in the life of the early church, between the death of Jesus and Paul's final imprisonment in Rome (63? 67?). This second book, presented here under the title of On Trial, is a continuation of Luke's Gospel. In the New Testament, it is called Acts of the Apostles. Luke was present at many of the events described in these pages. He was one of Paul's companions on at least some of his journeys. (You may notice some shifting between "we" and "they" in the later chapters of the book.)

Luke dedicated both his Gospel and his Acts of the Apostles to a man named Theophilus (the name means "one who loves God"). Luke addressed him as "Most Excellent," which was the way high Roman officials were addressed. Theophilus may have sponsored Luke's writings and arranged to have copies of them sent to Greek-speaking Christian communities. There is a tradition that Luke never married and that he lived till the age of 84.

St. Luke's feast day is October 18.

About Paul the Apostle

WHEN PAUL WAS MIRACULOUSLY CONVERTED on the road to Damascus, there remained some 30 to 35 years of his life. By the time of his death, and largely through his efforts, the fledgling Christian sect had spread to every corner of the then-known world.

Paul must have had a will of iron—and the constitution of a marathon runner. For three decades, he endured almost constant hardship, traveling extensively, often under dangerous circumstances. He was no stranger to insults, threats, and beatings. He was frequently put in jail. Once Paul had become a missionary for the Christ whose followers he had formerly persecuted, nothing short of death could stop him. Whether at liberty or in prison, Paul wrote letters of encouragement to the Christian communities in Galatia, Thessalonica, Rome, Ephesus, Philippi, and Colossae. These letters became books of the New Testament, as did his letters to Philemon, Timothy, and Titus—leaders of Christian communities.

St. Paul's feast day is January 25.

98